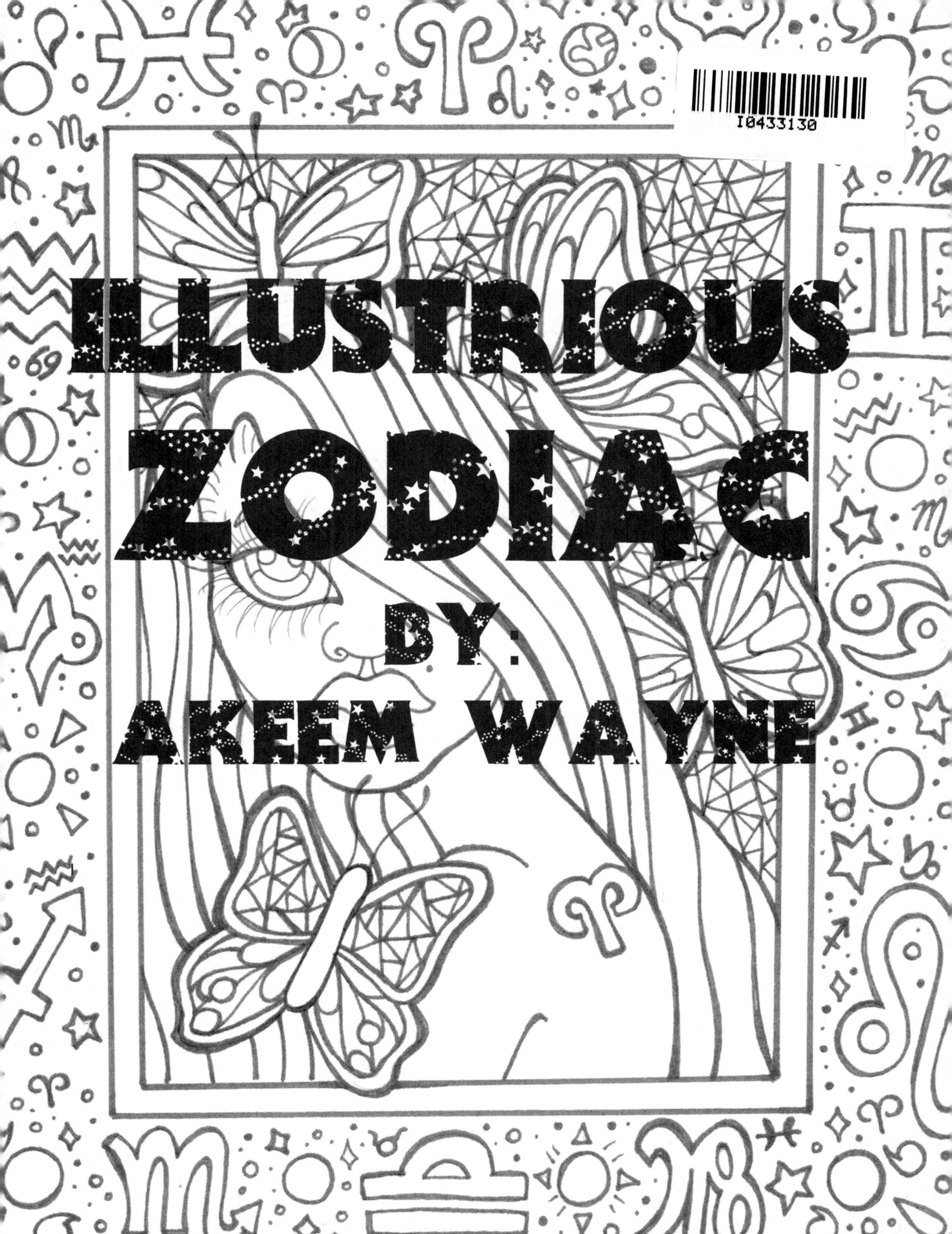

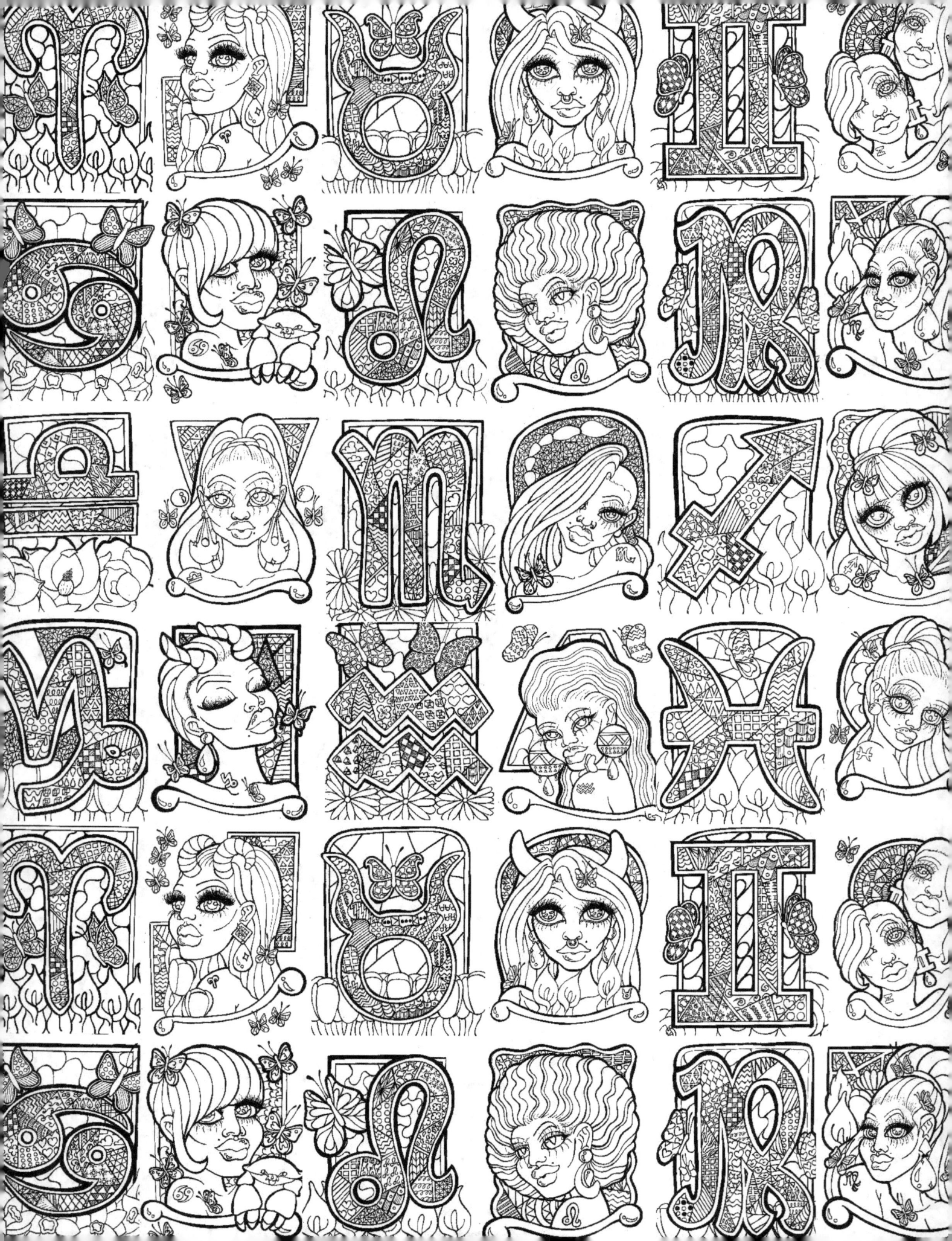

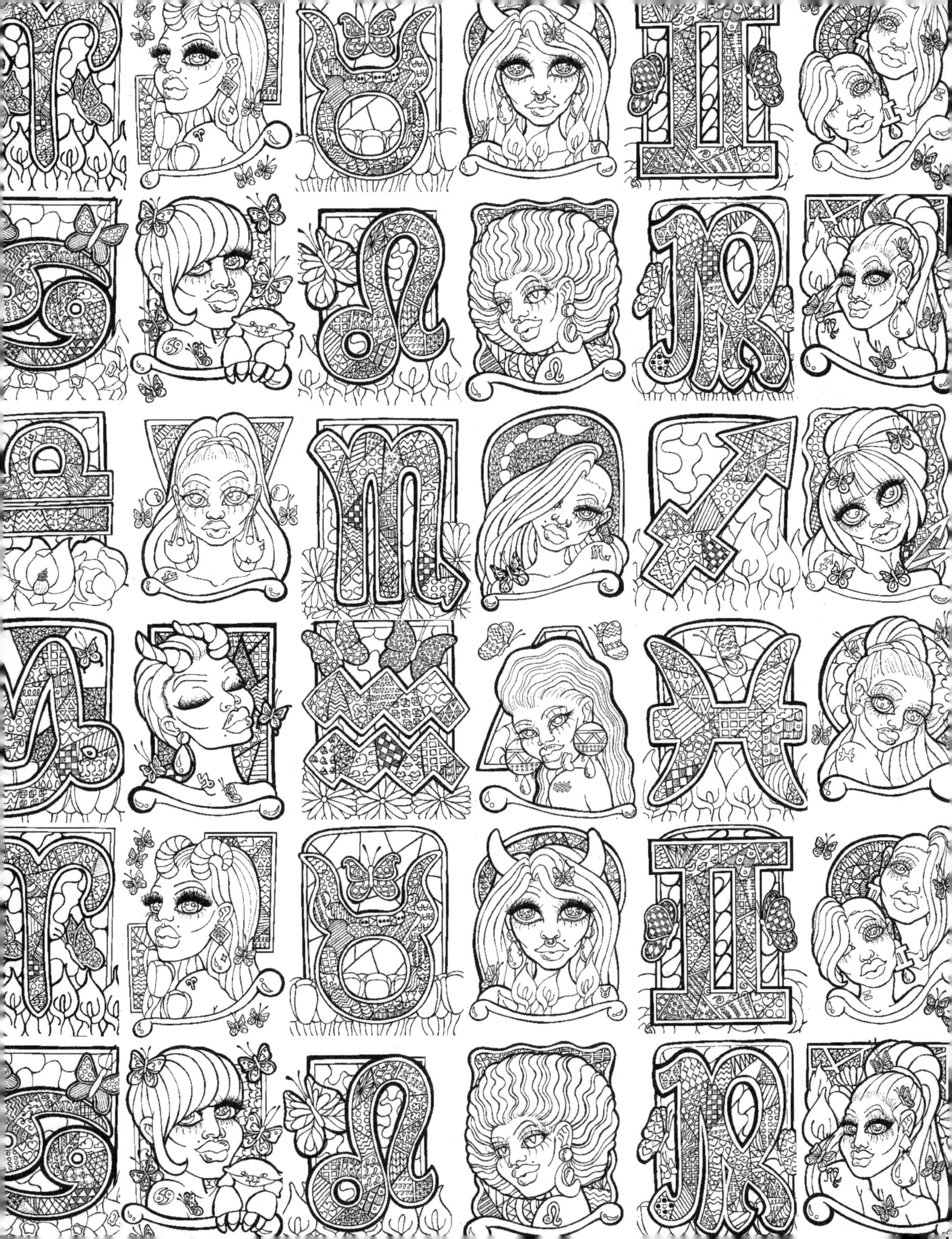

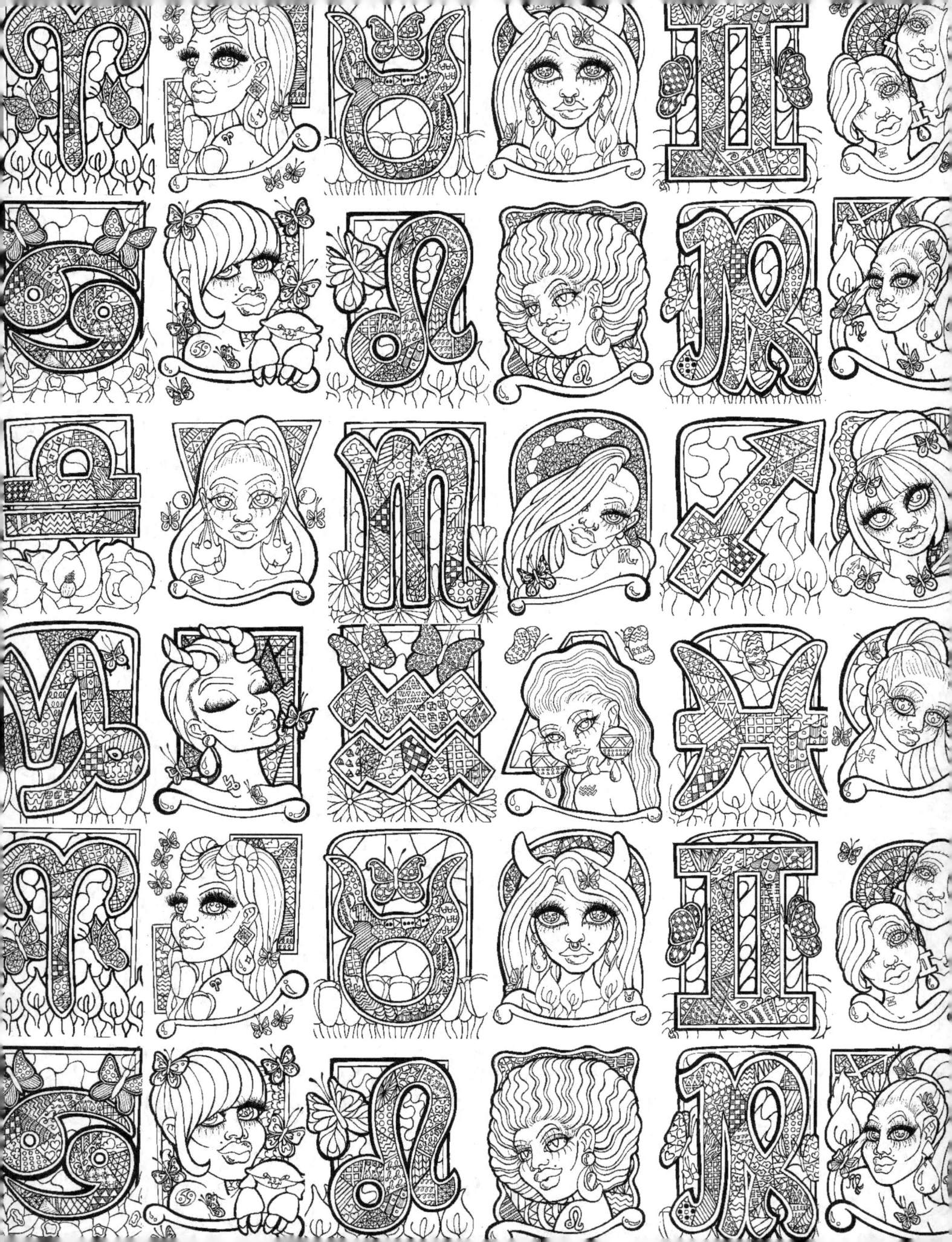

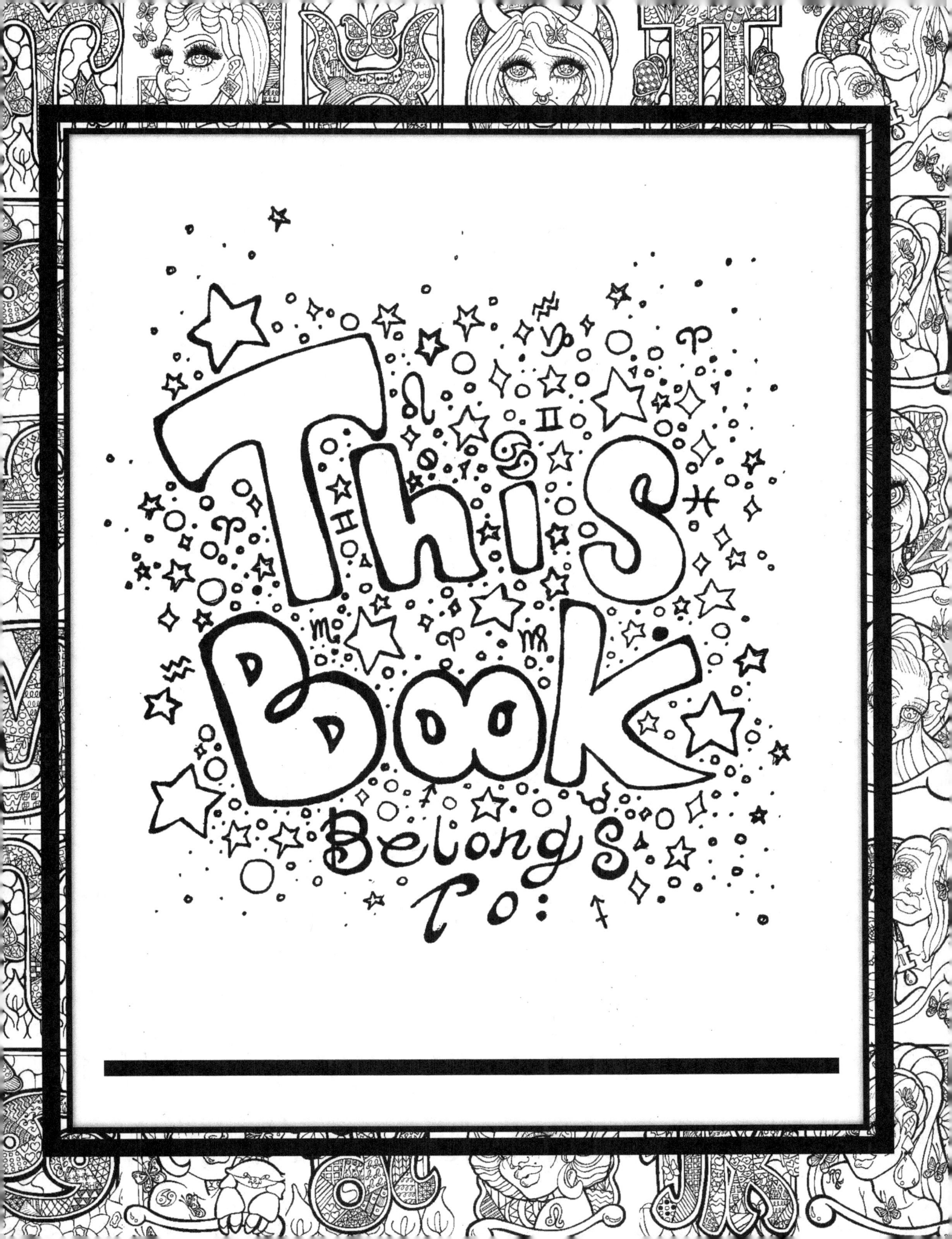

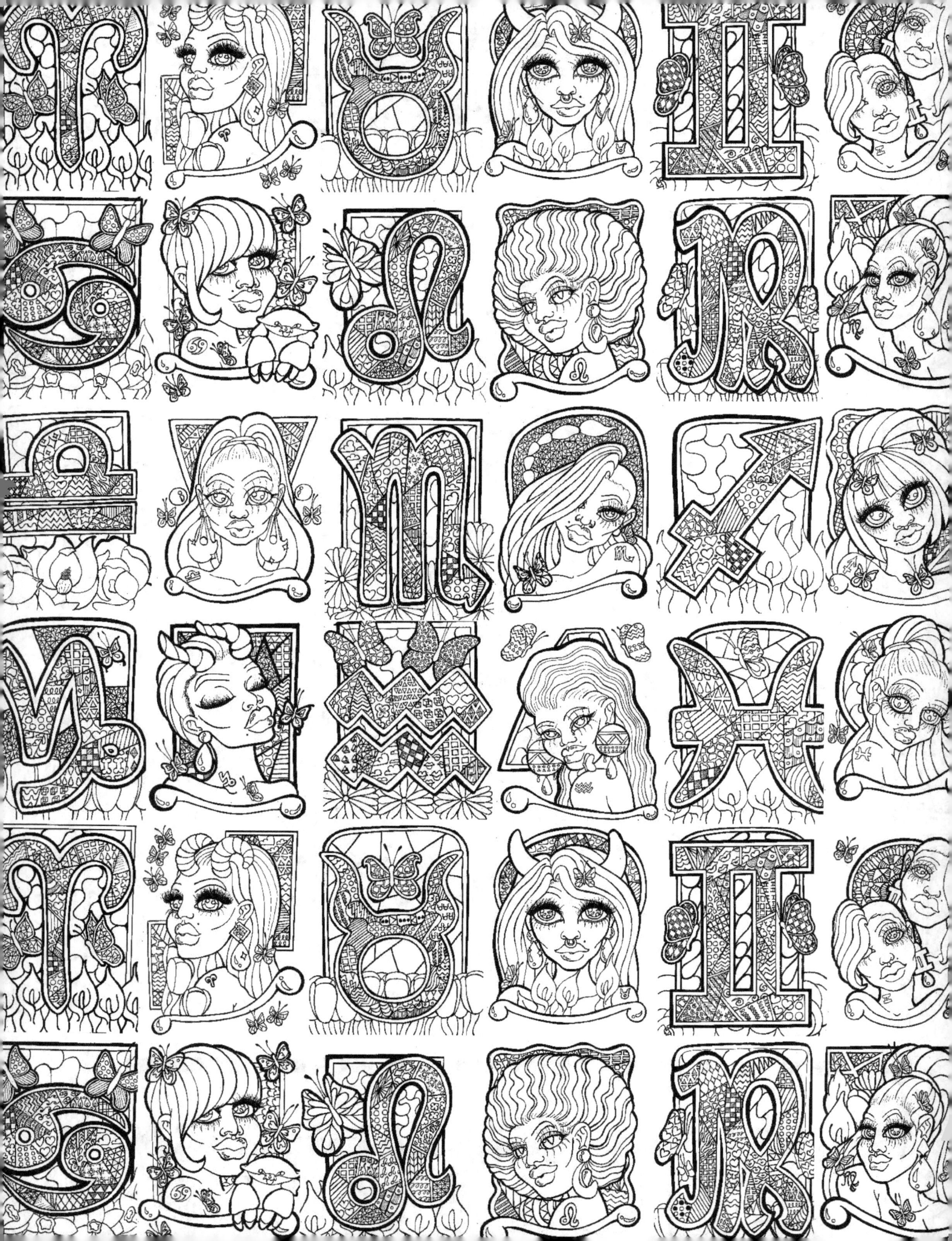

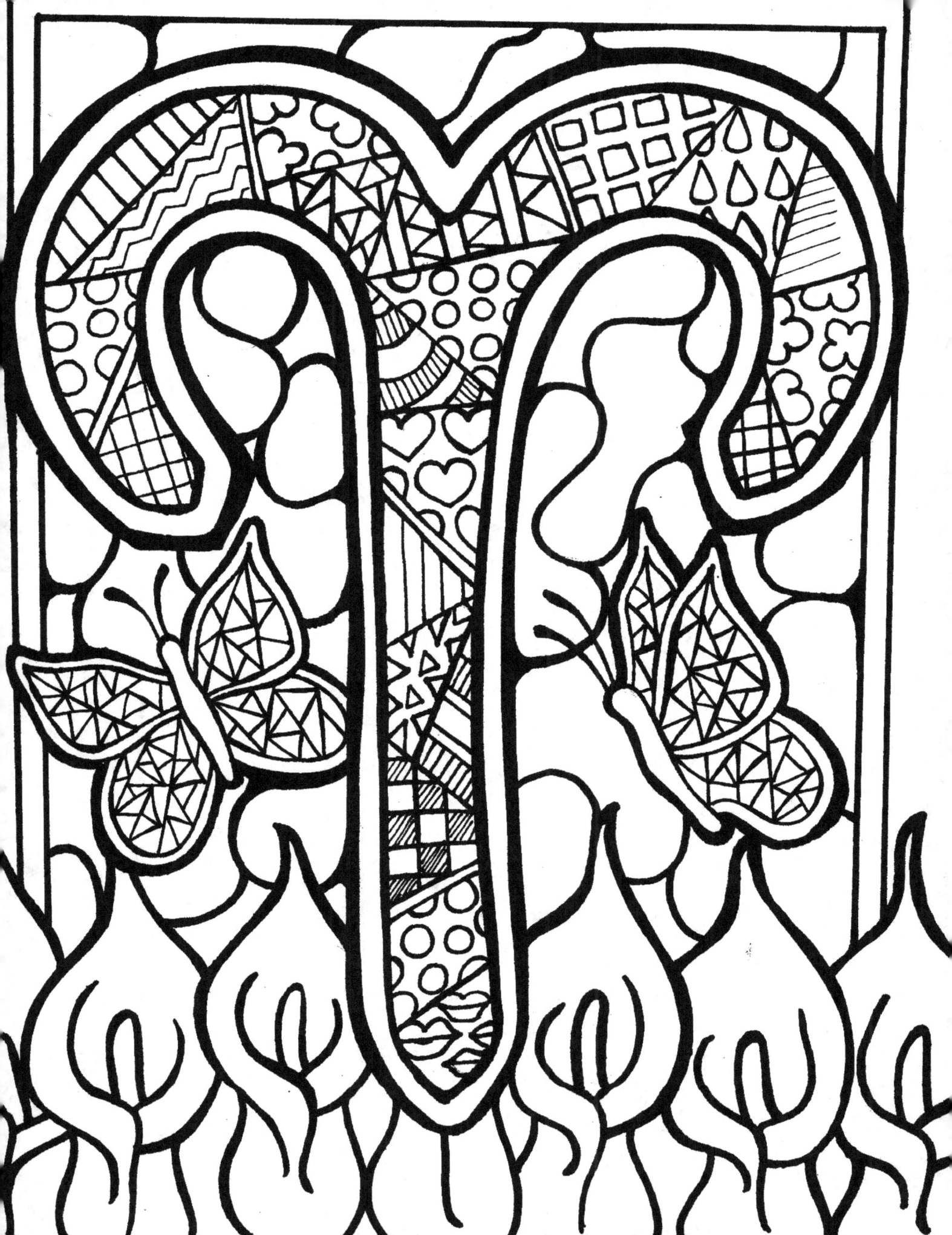

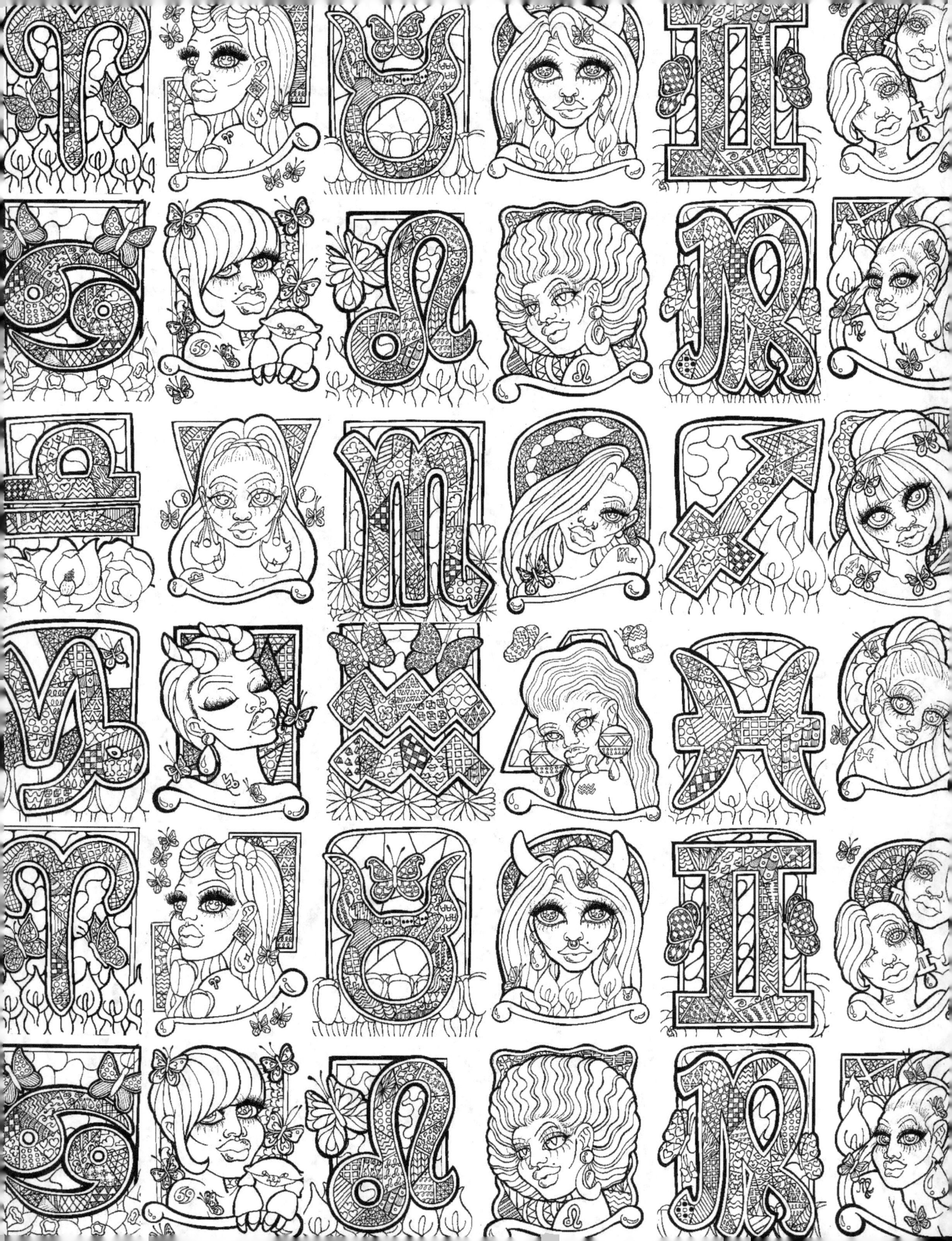

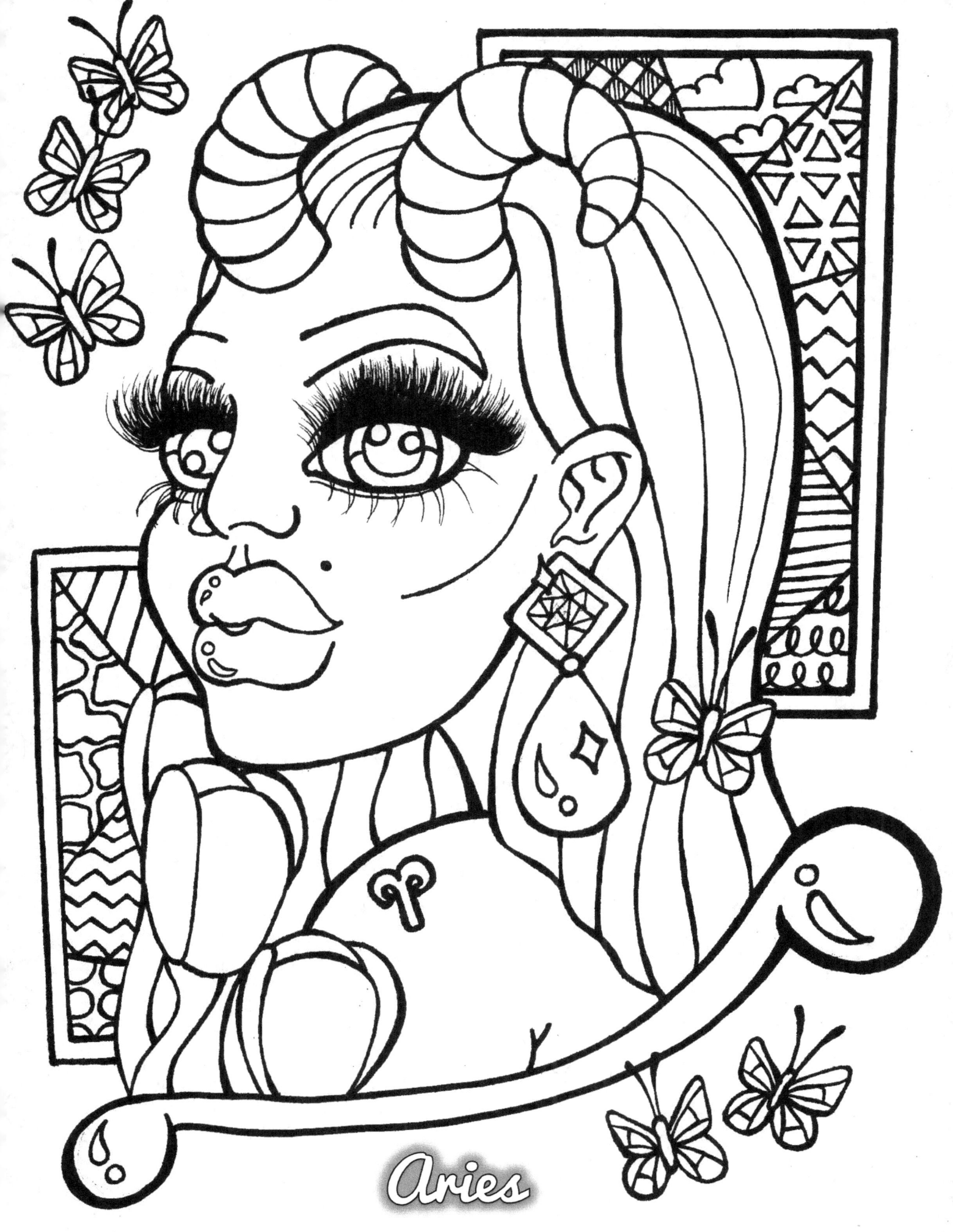

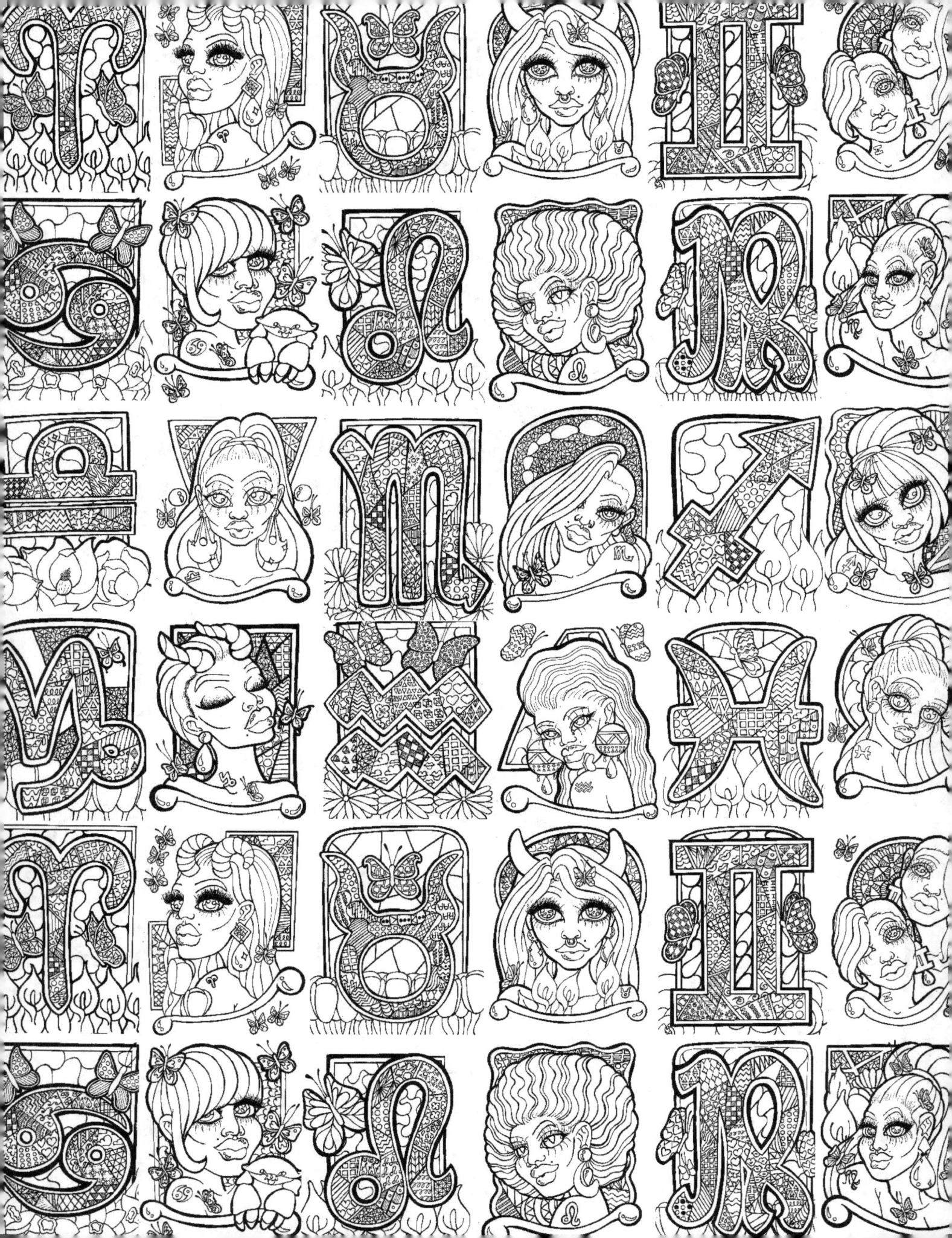

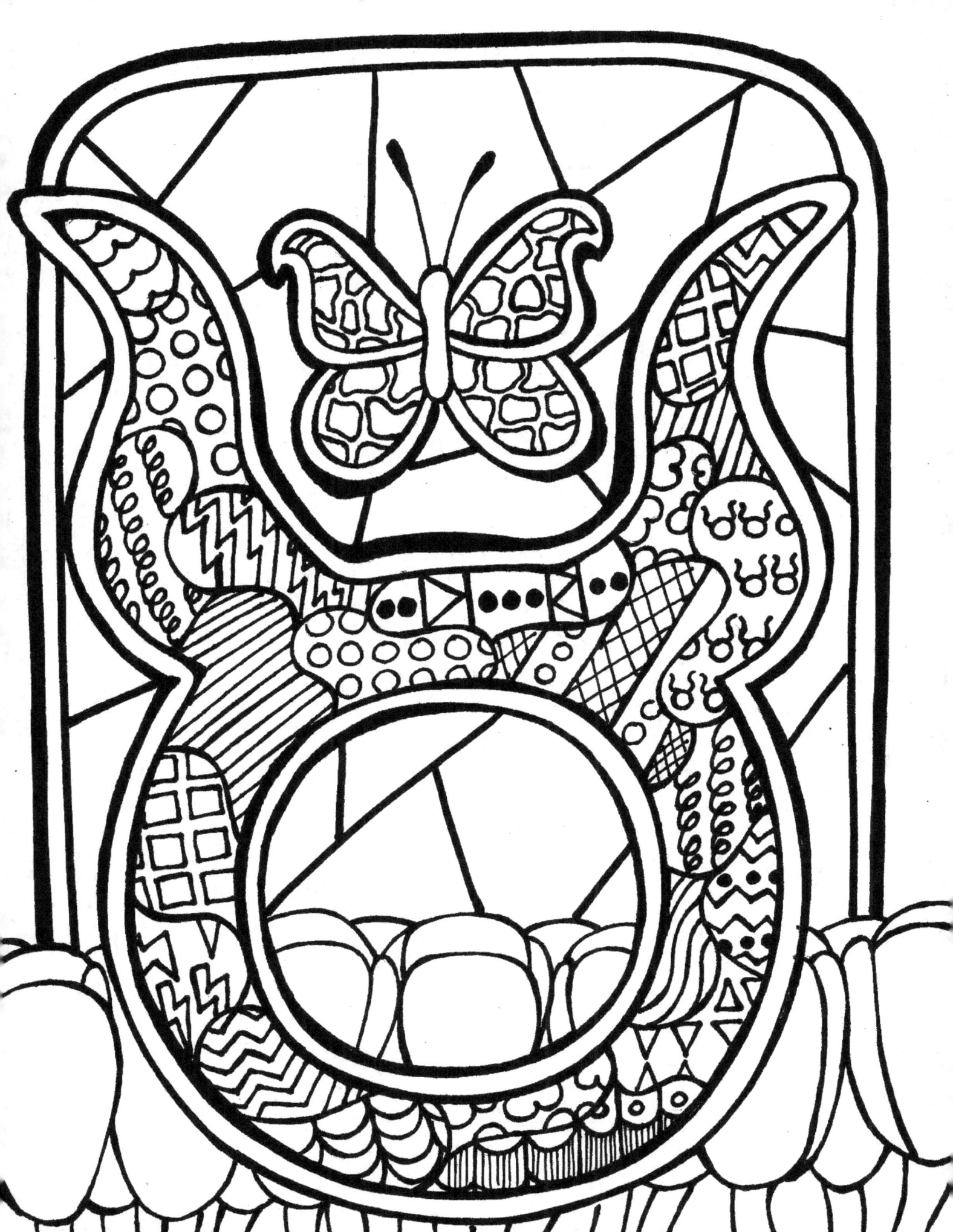

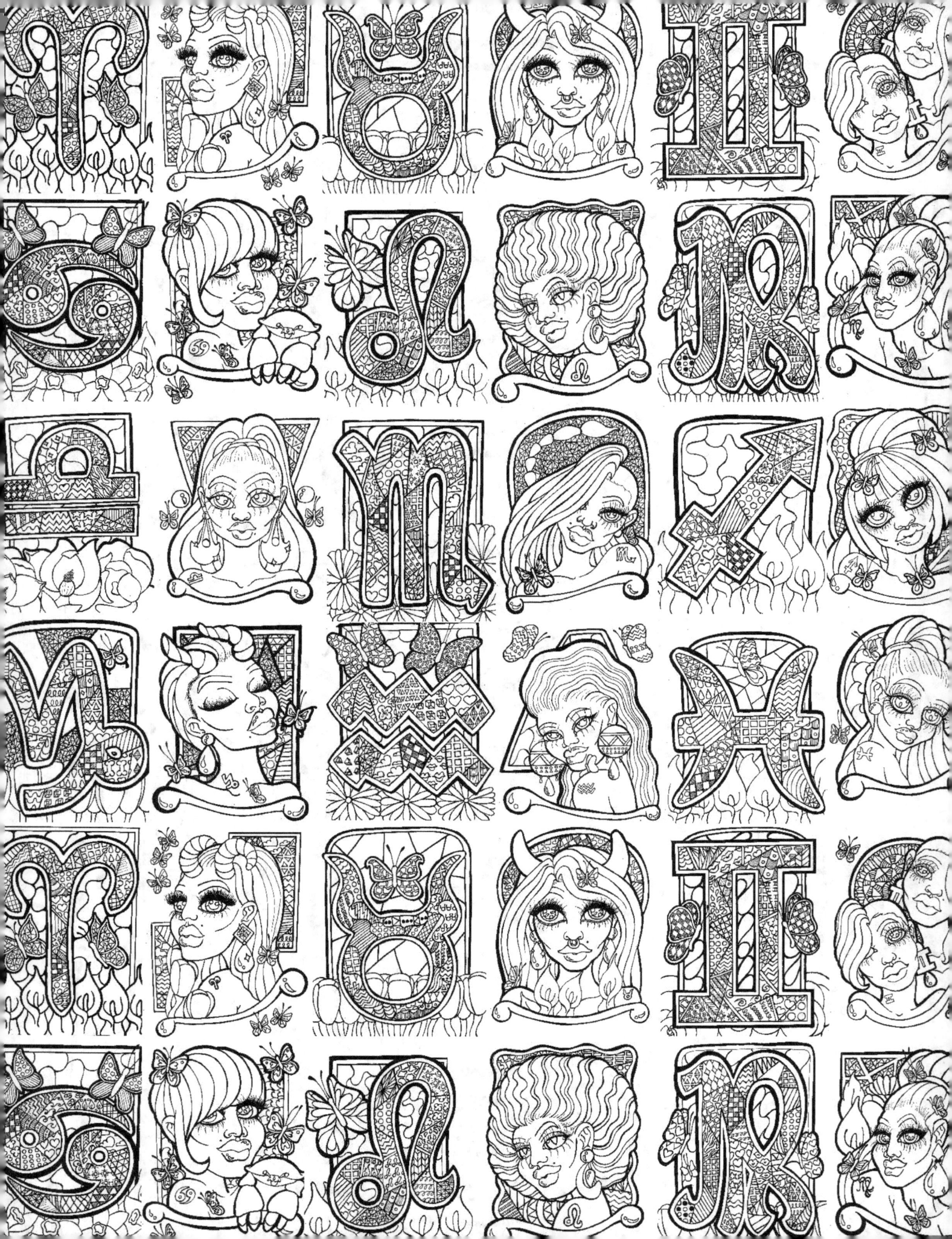

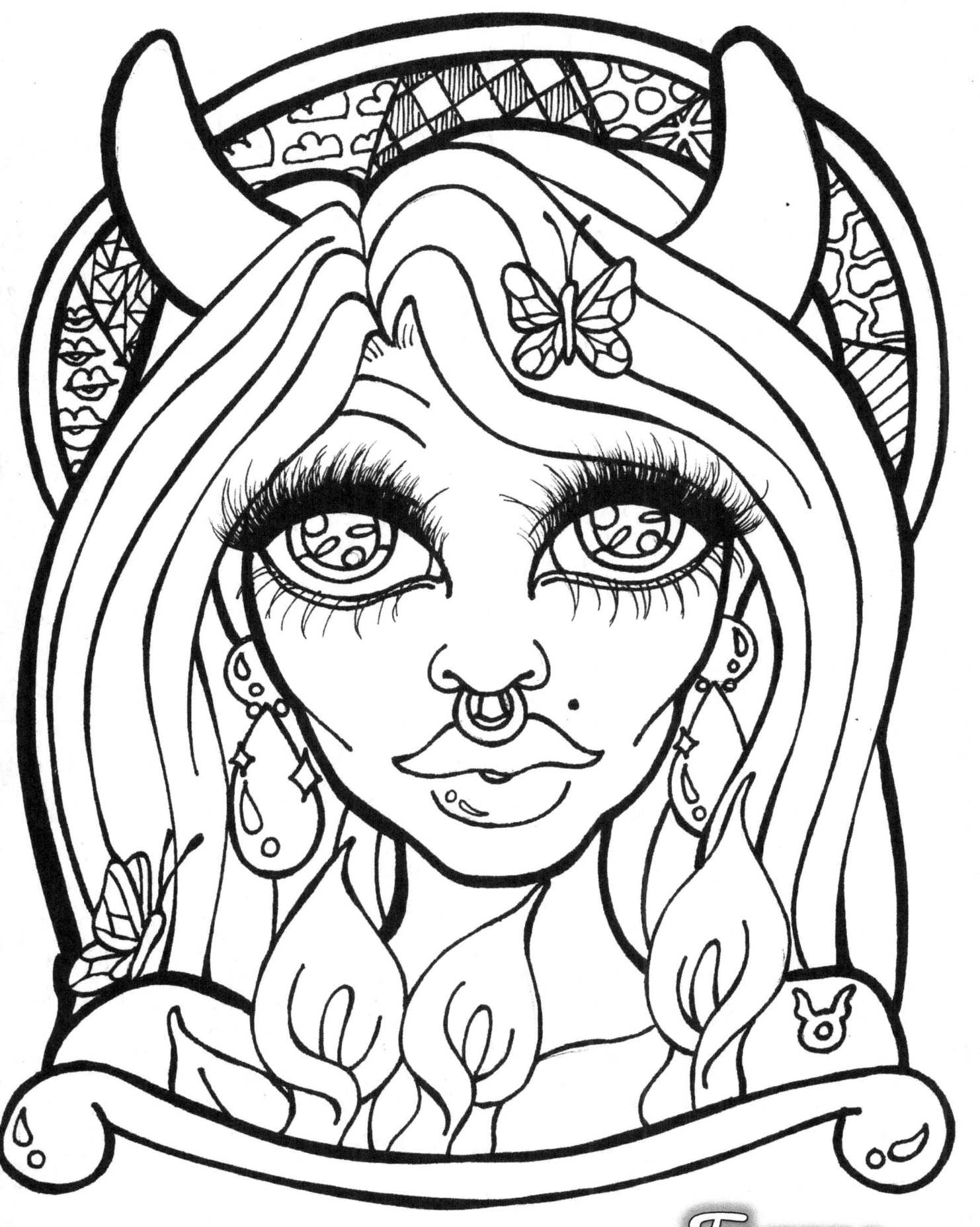

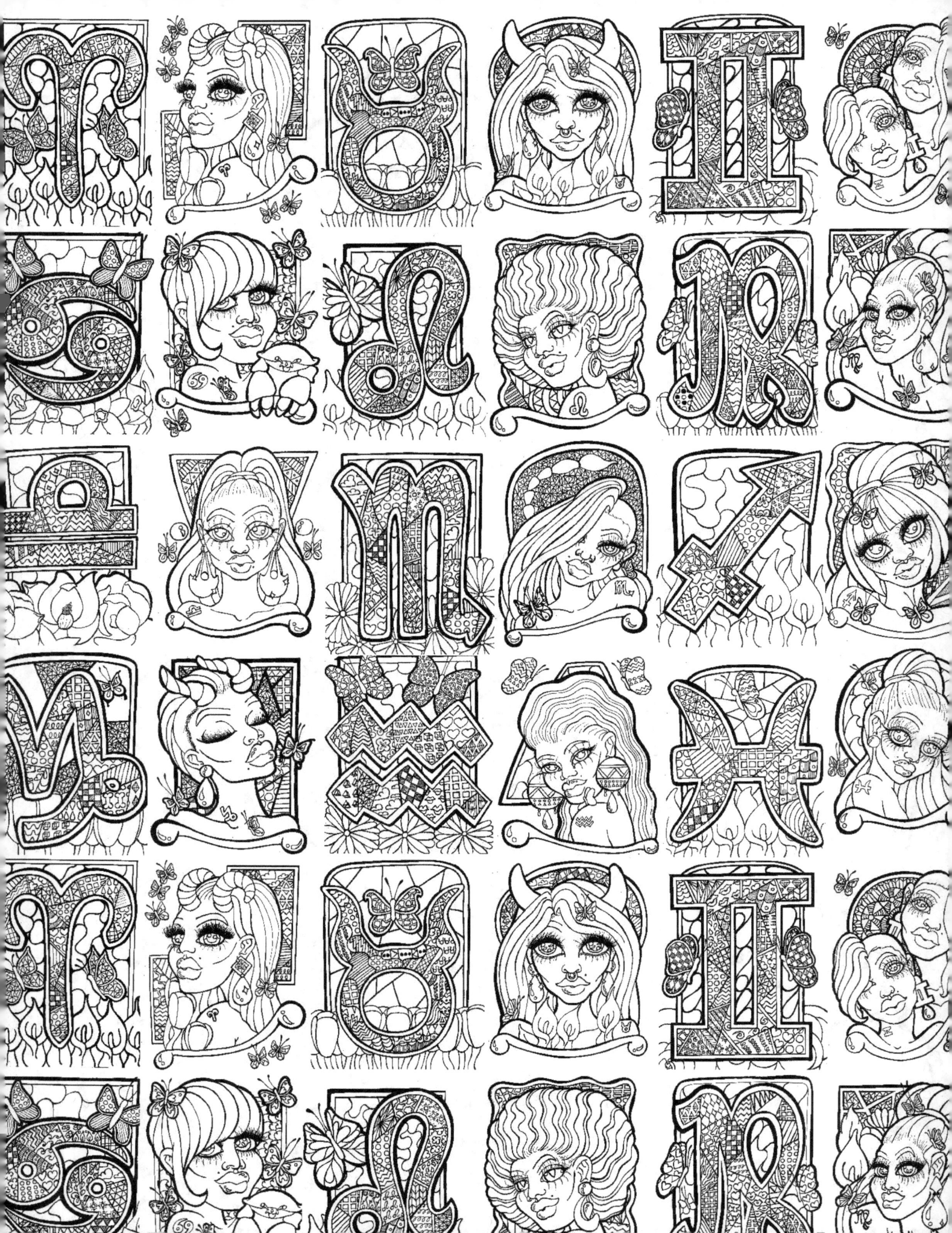

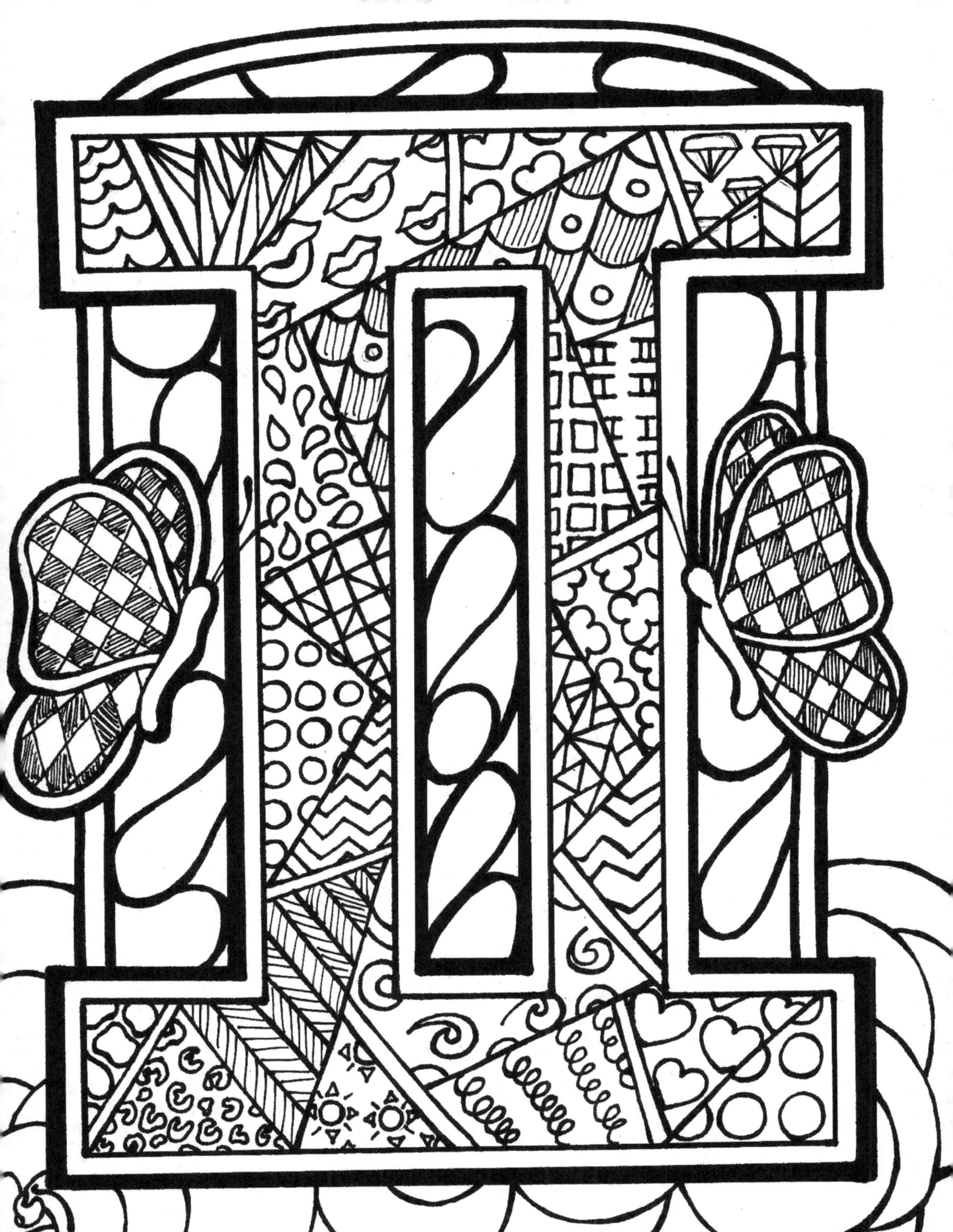

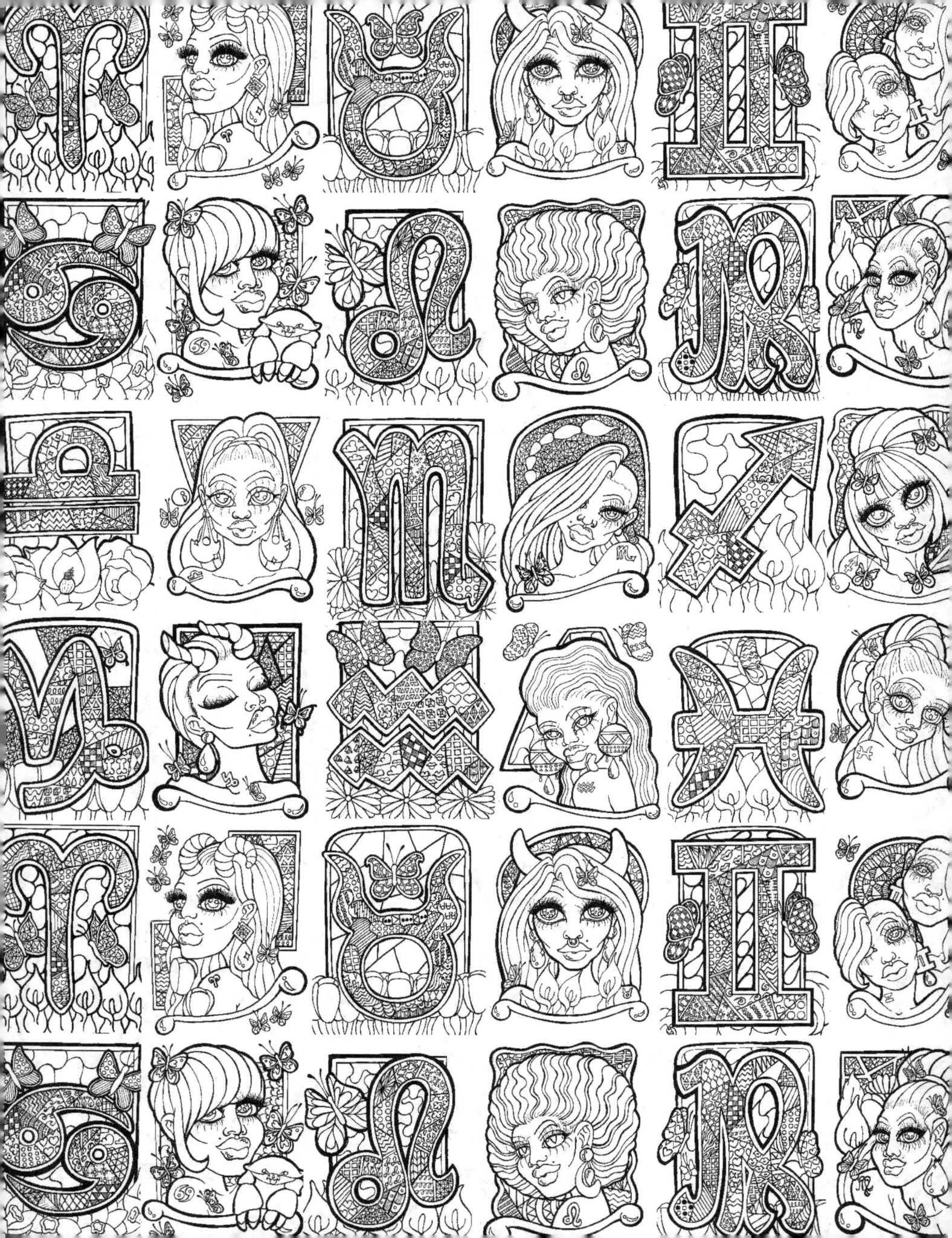

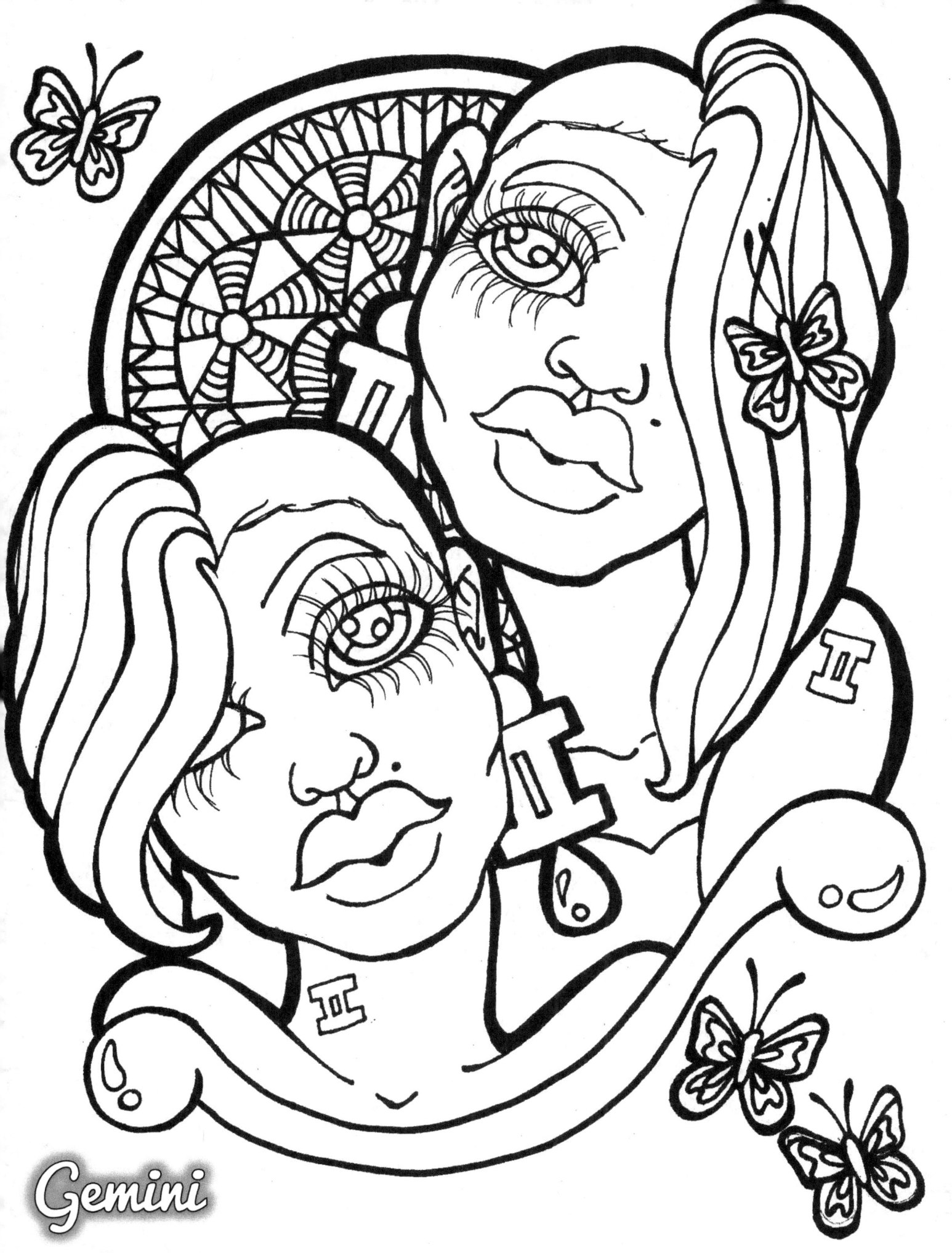

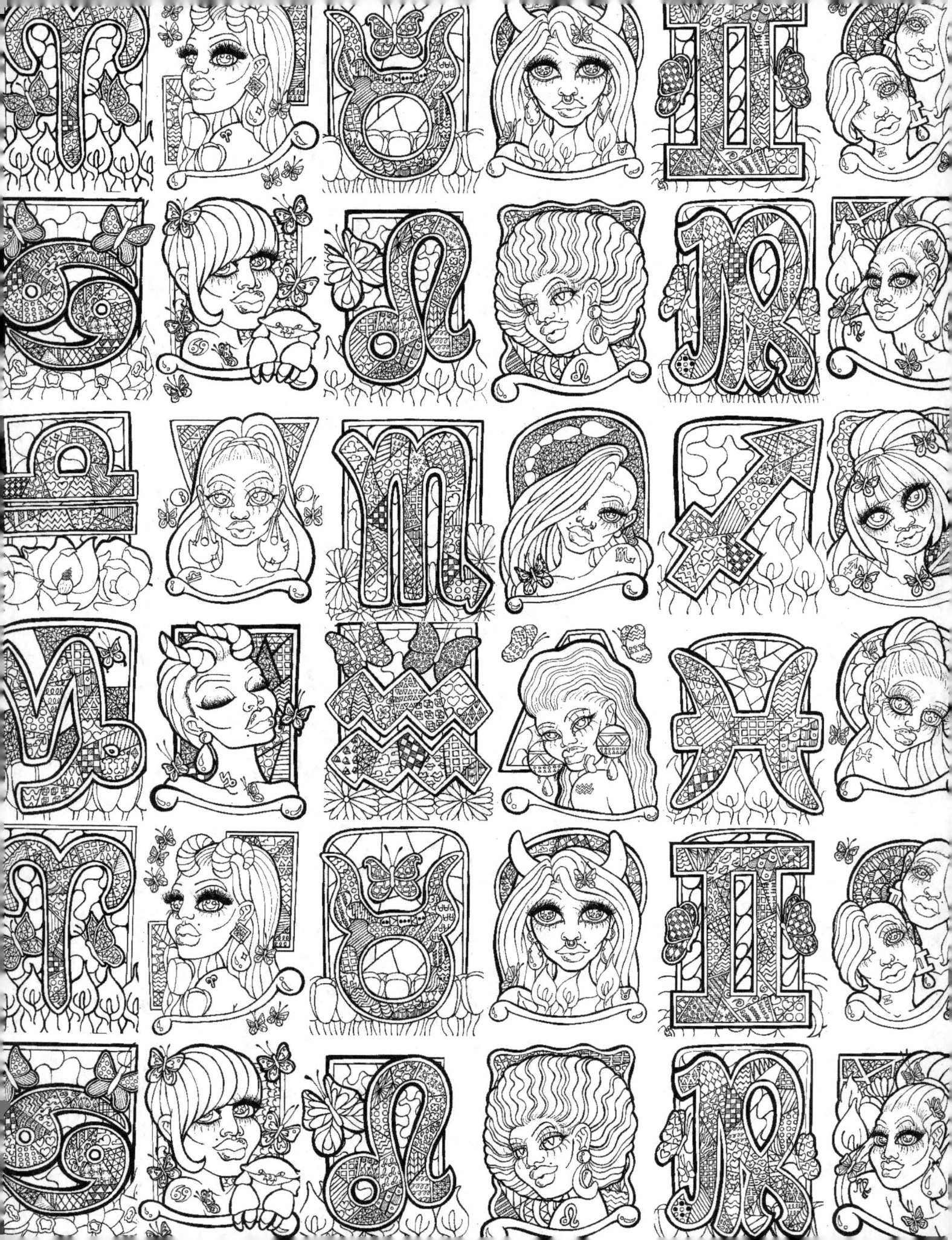

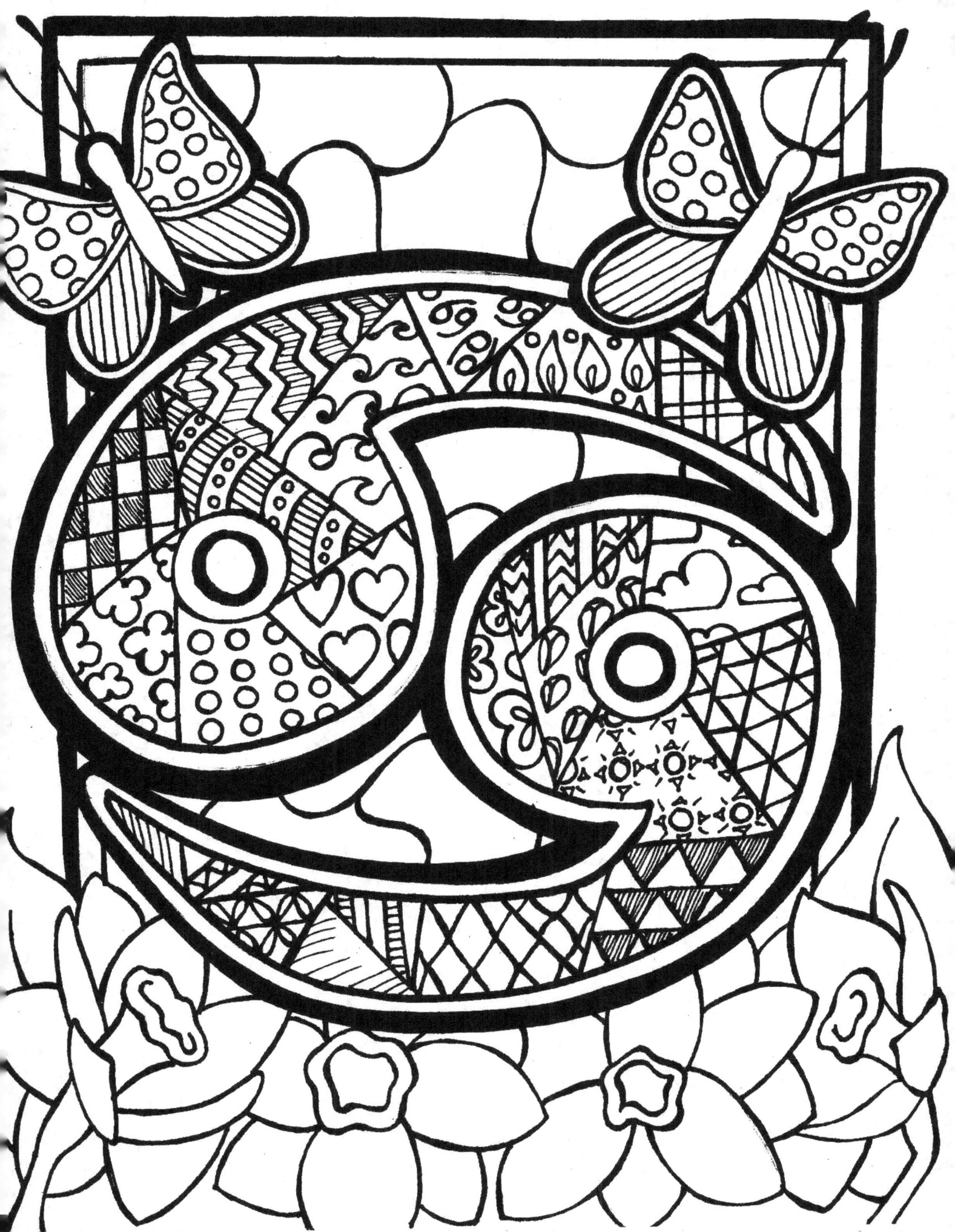

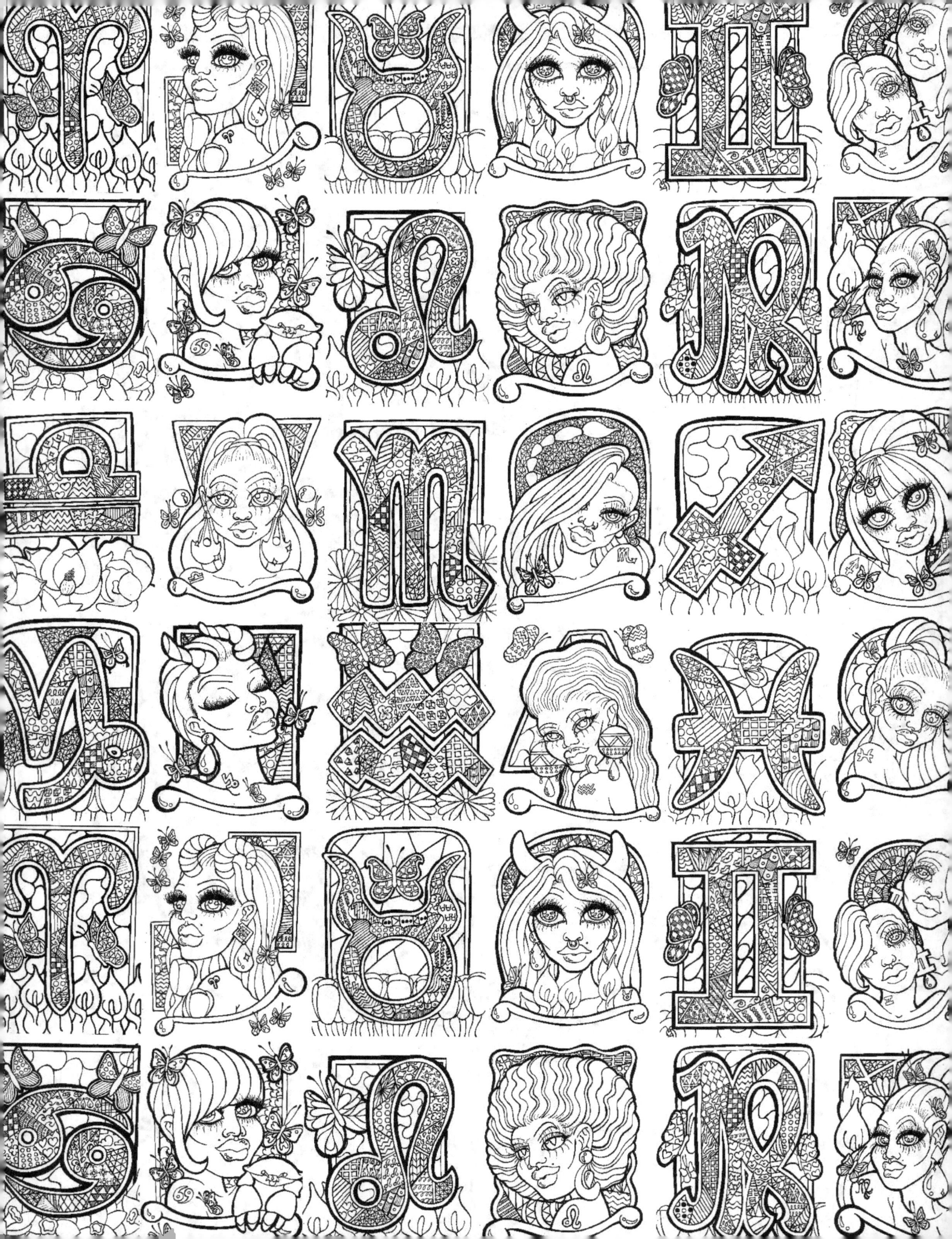

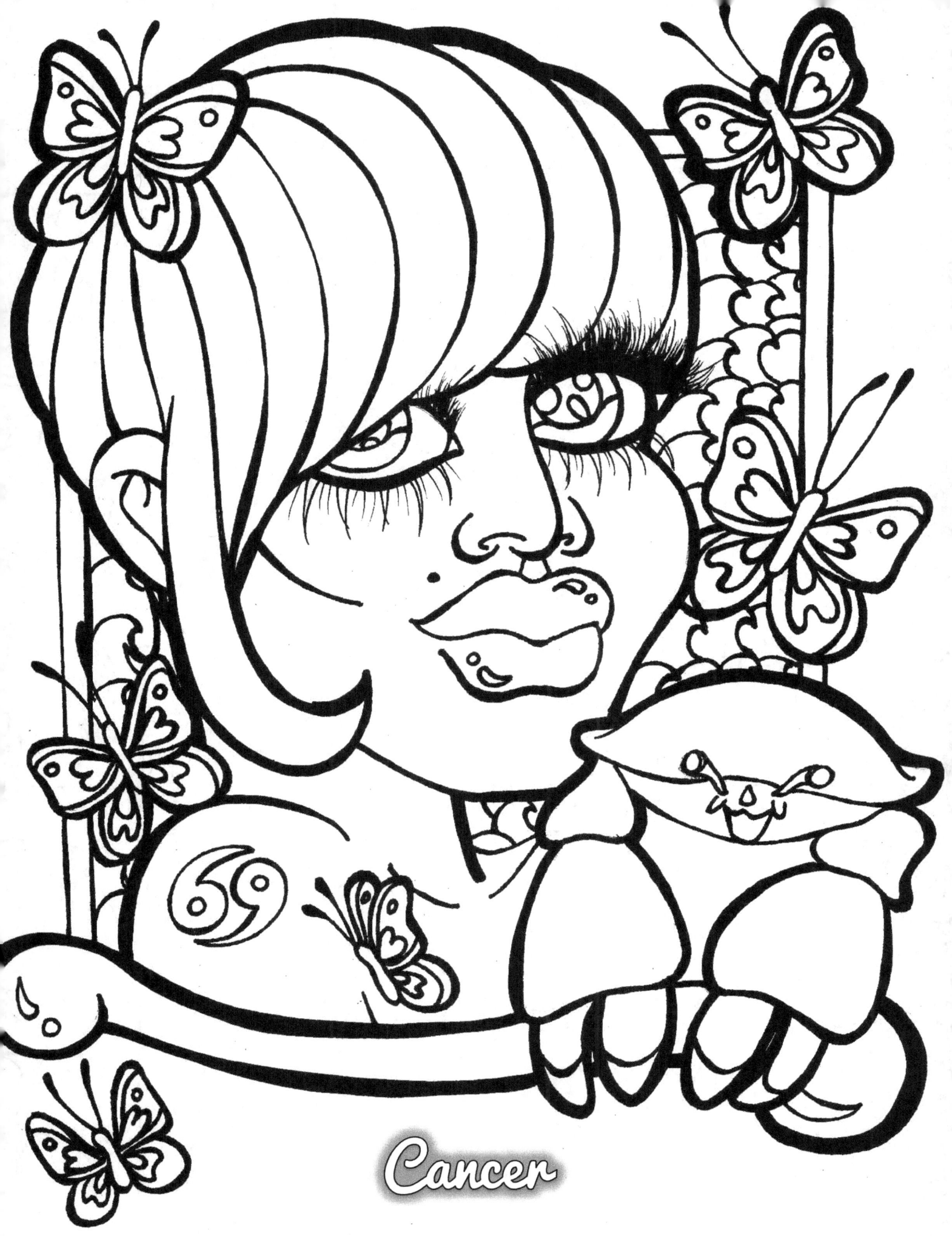

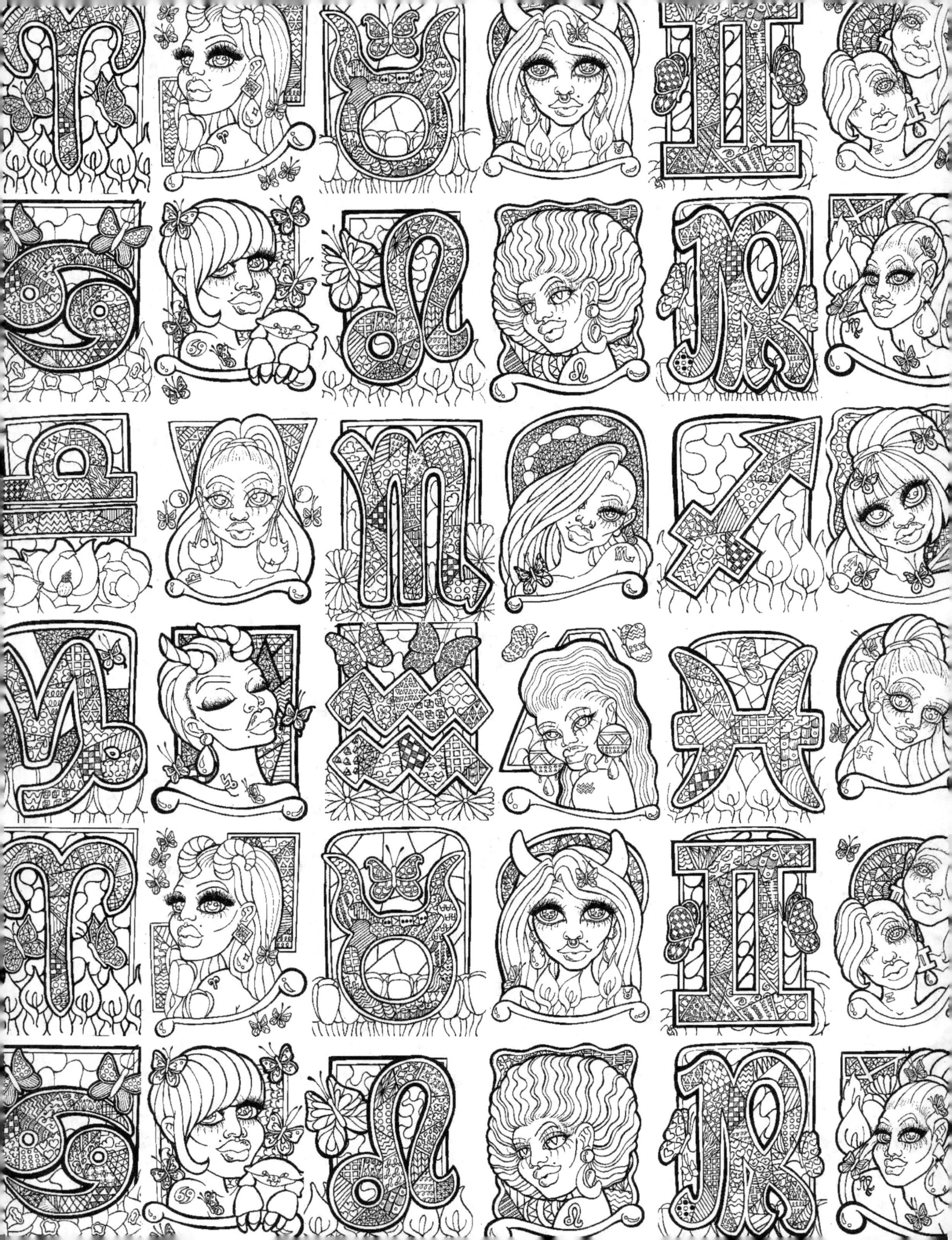

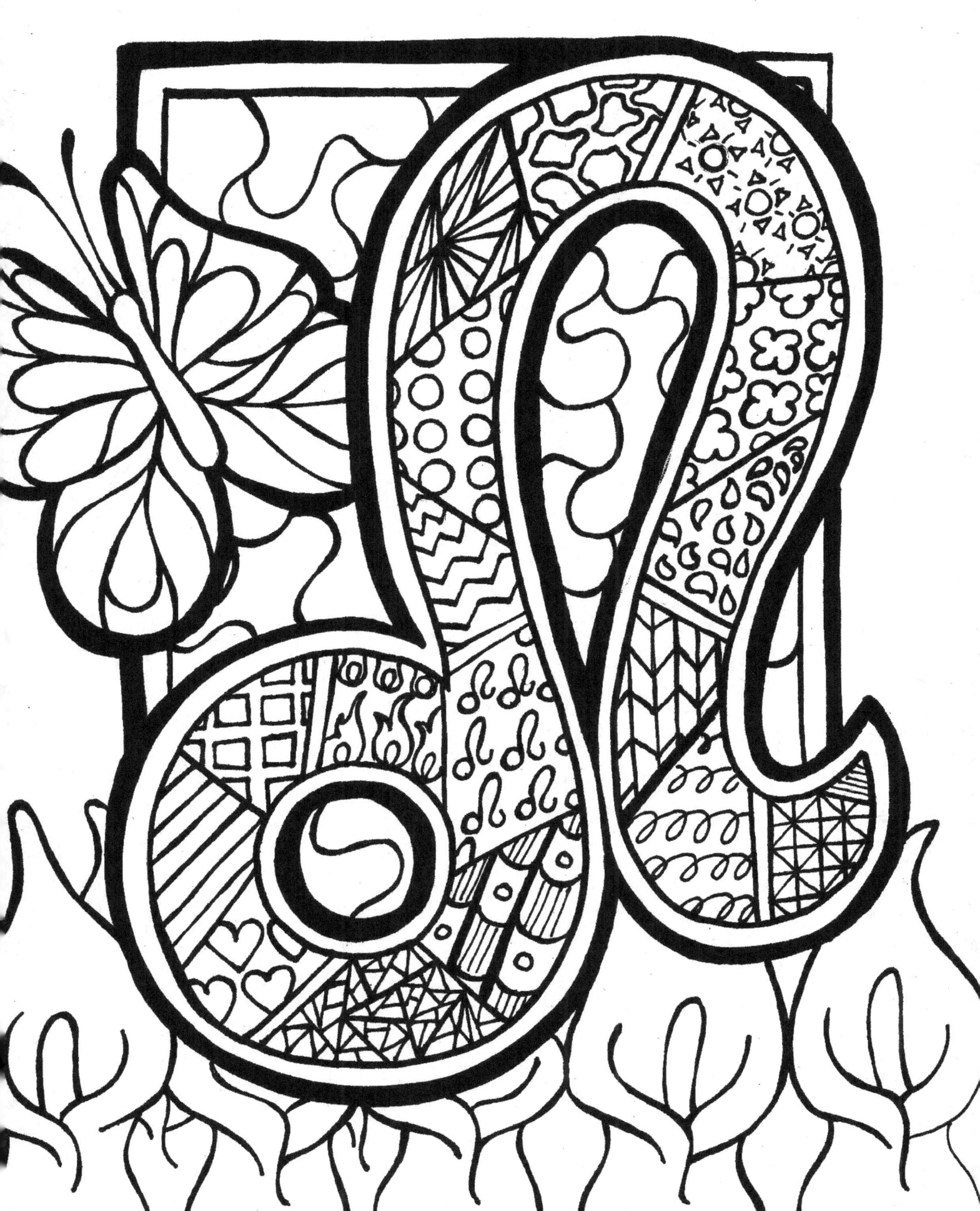

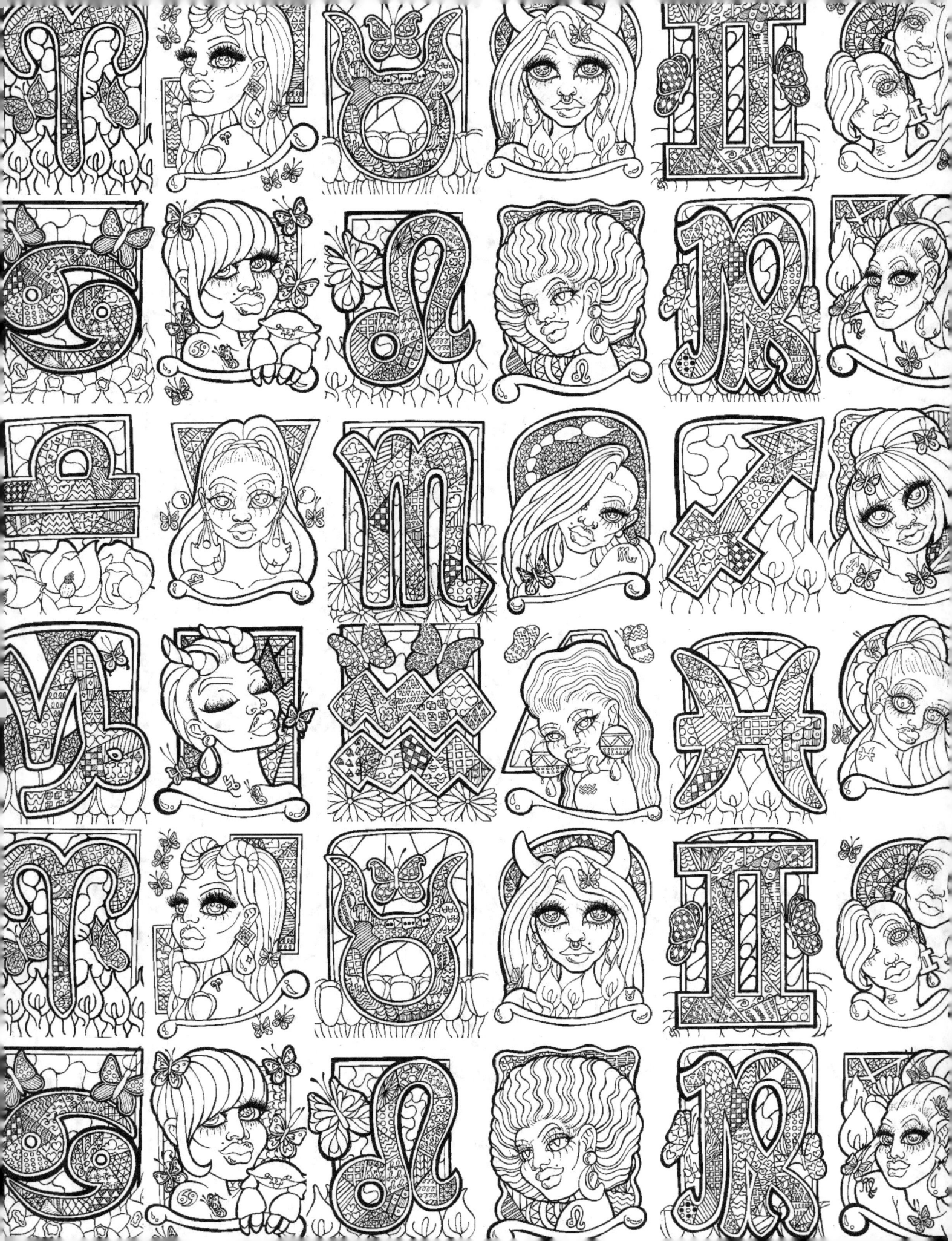

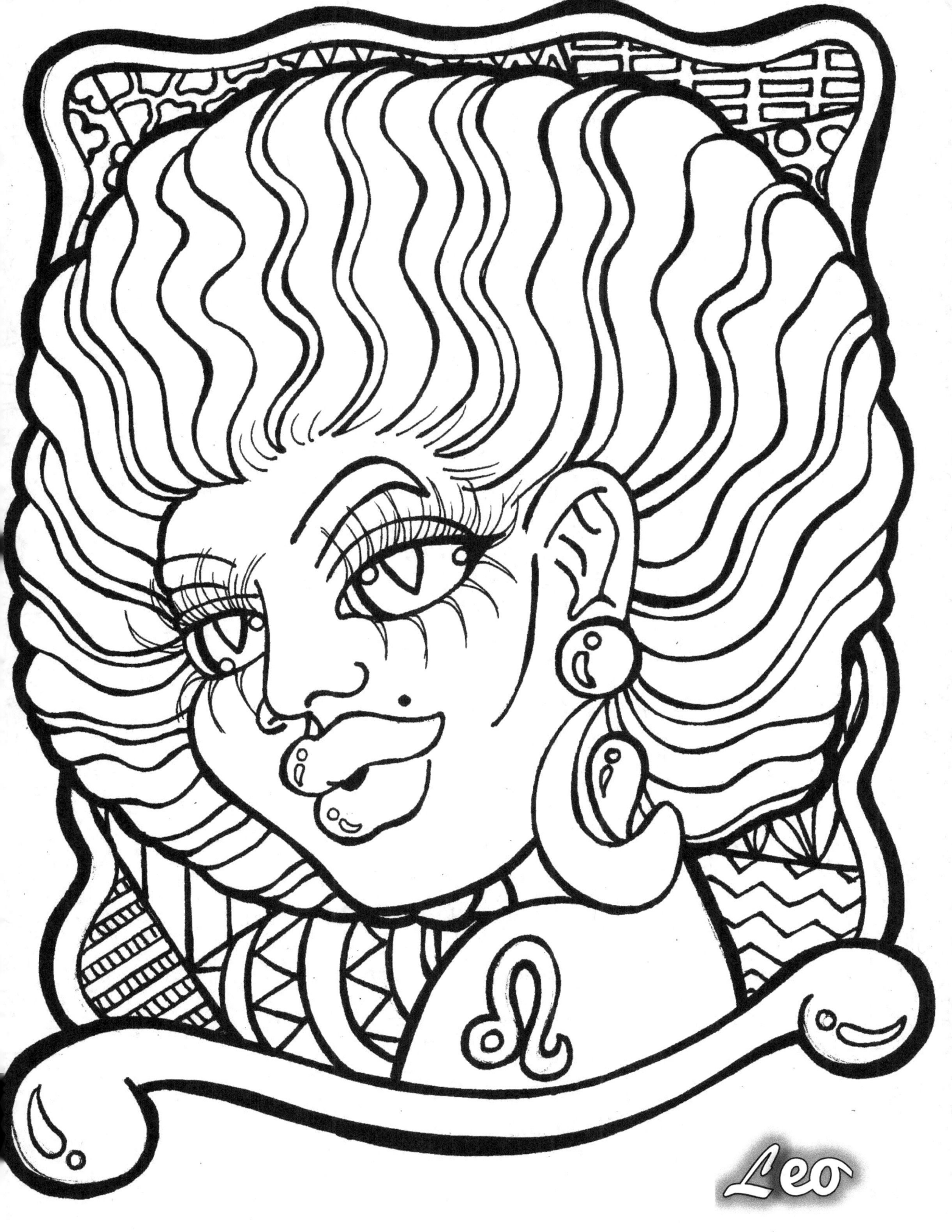

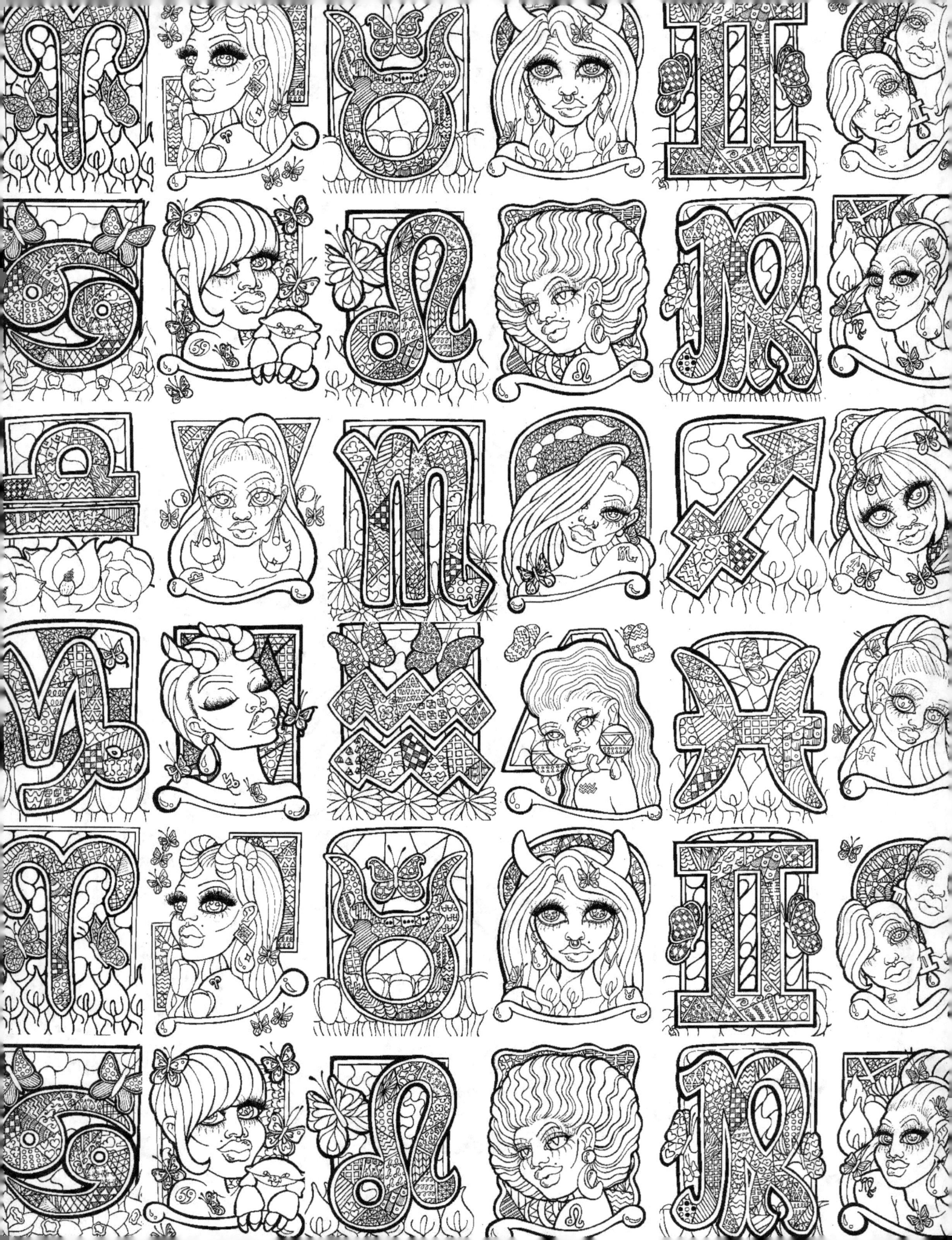

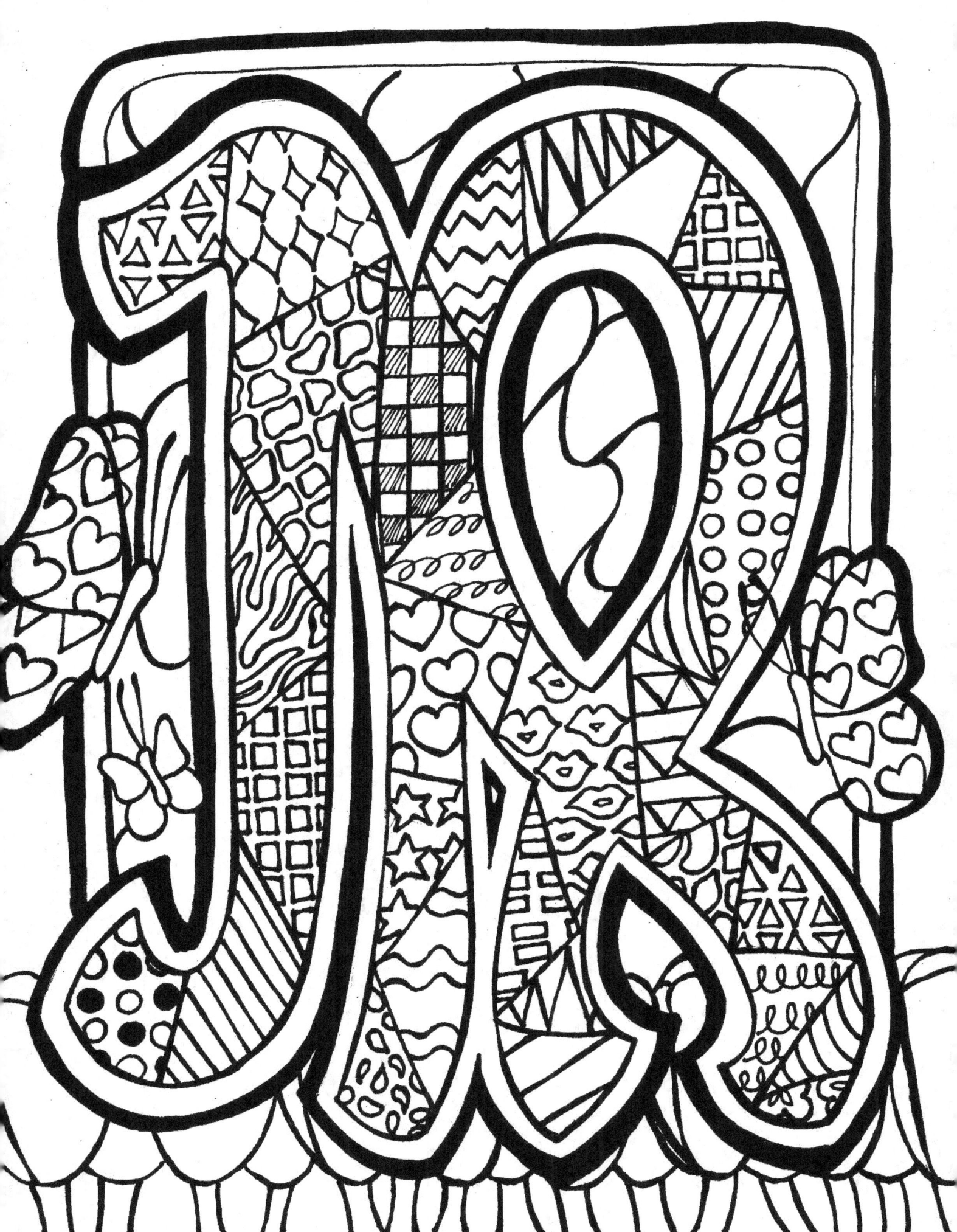

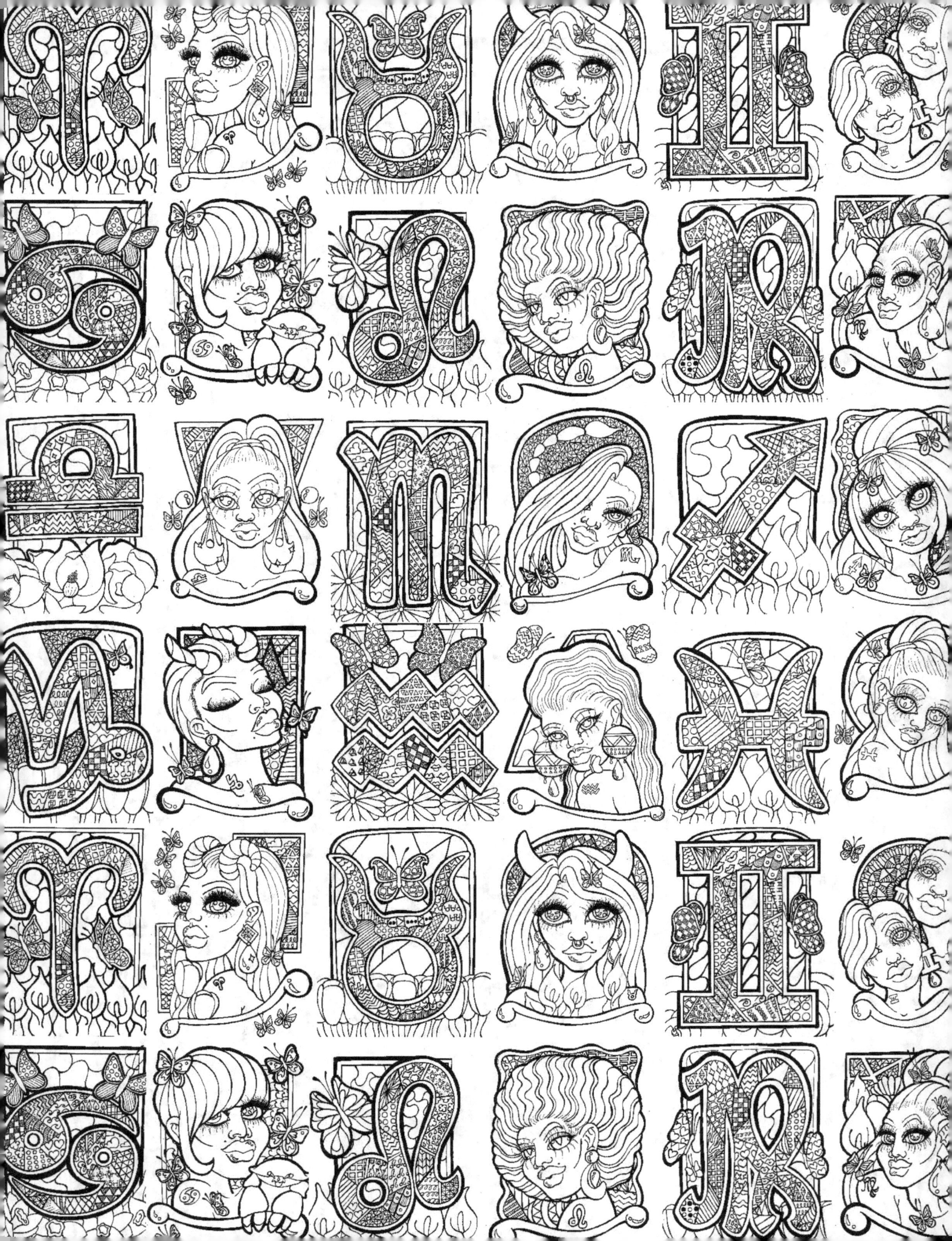

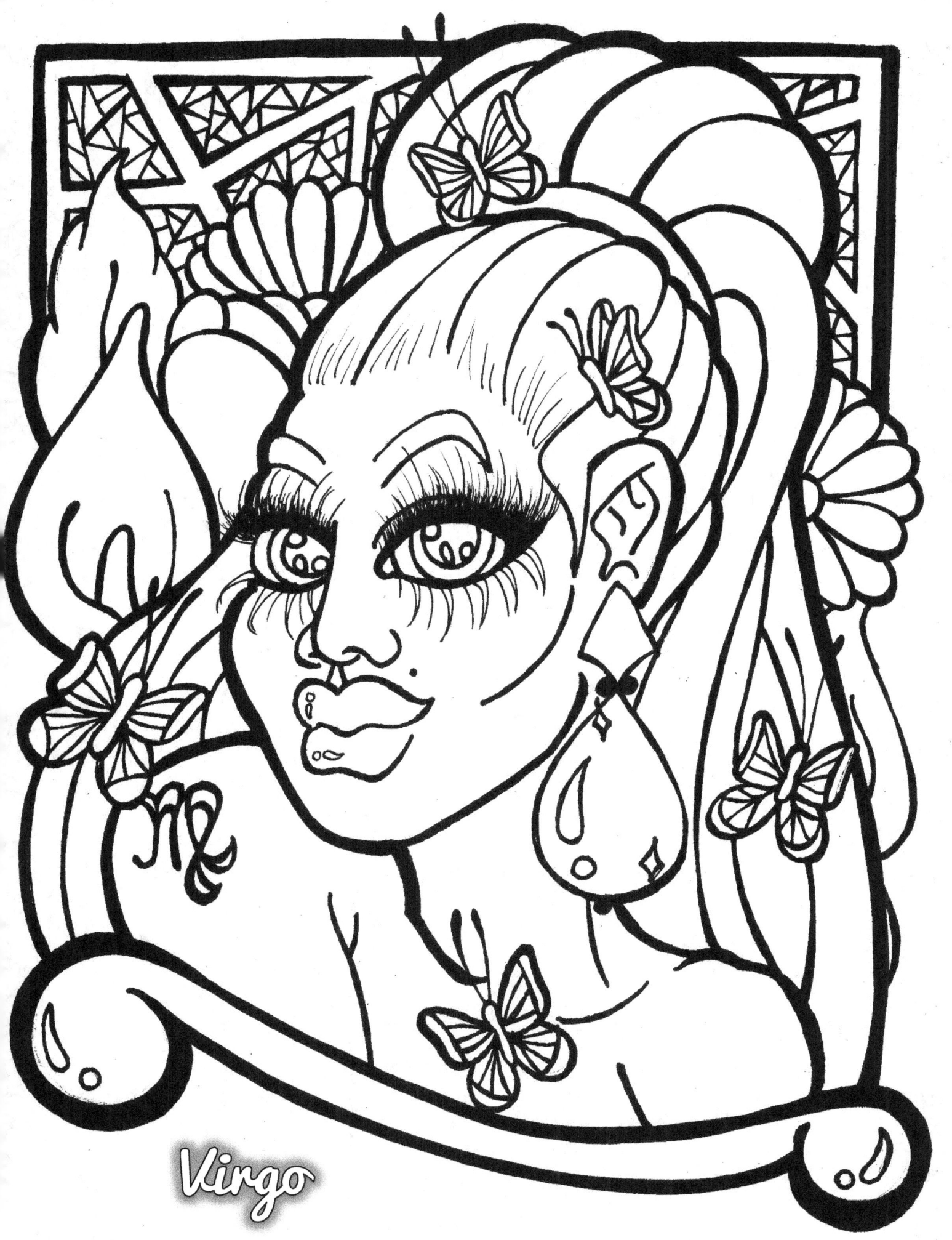

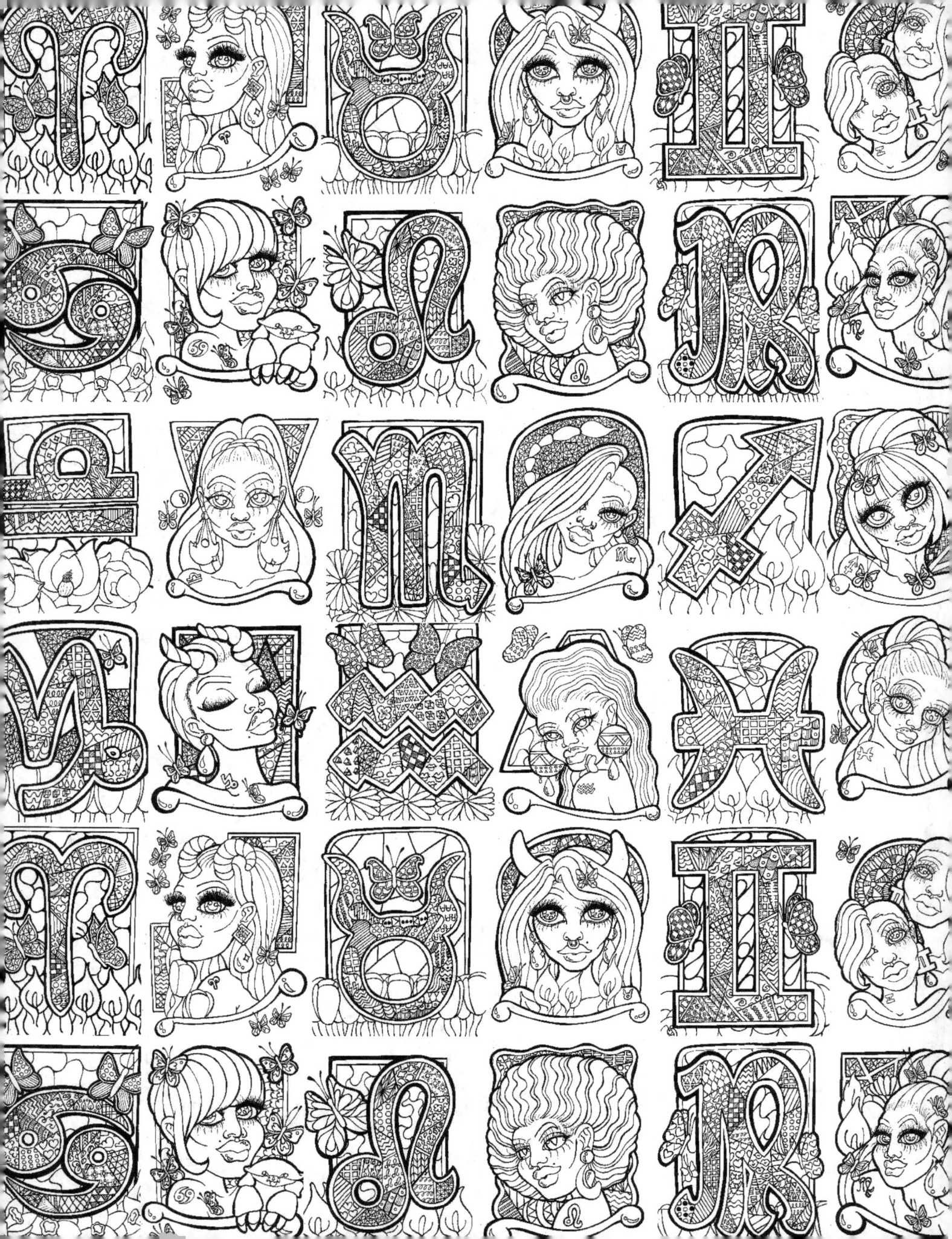

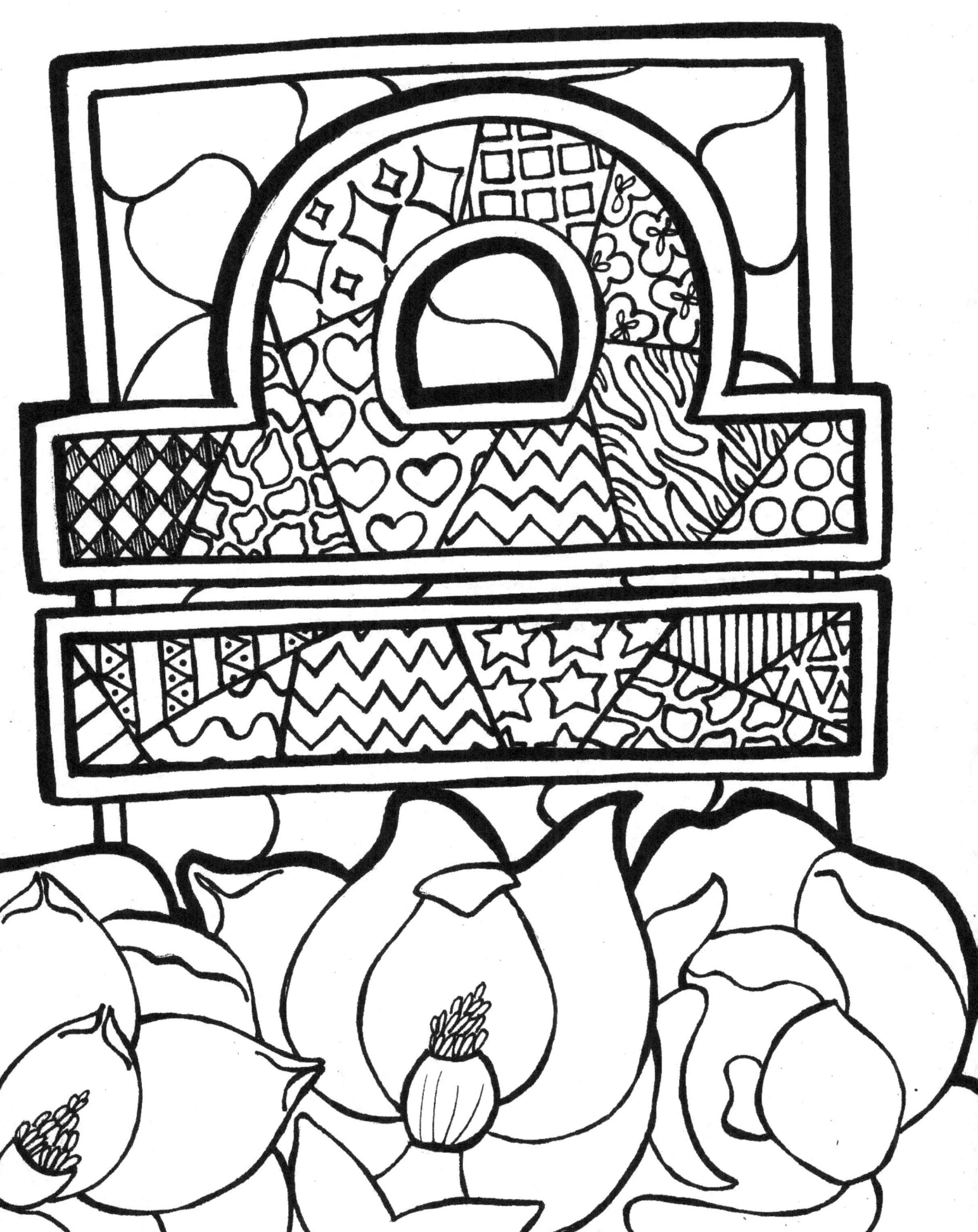

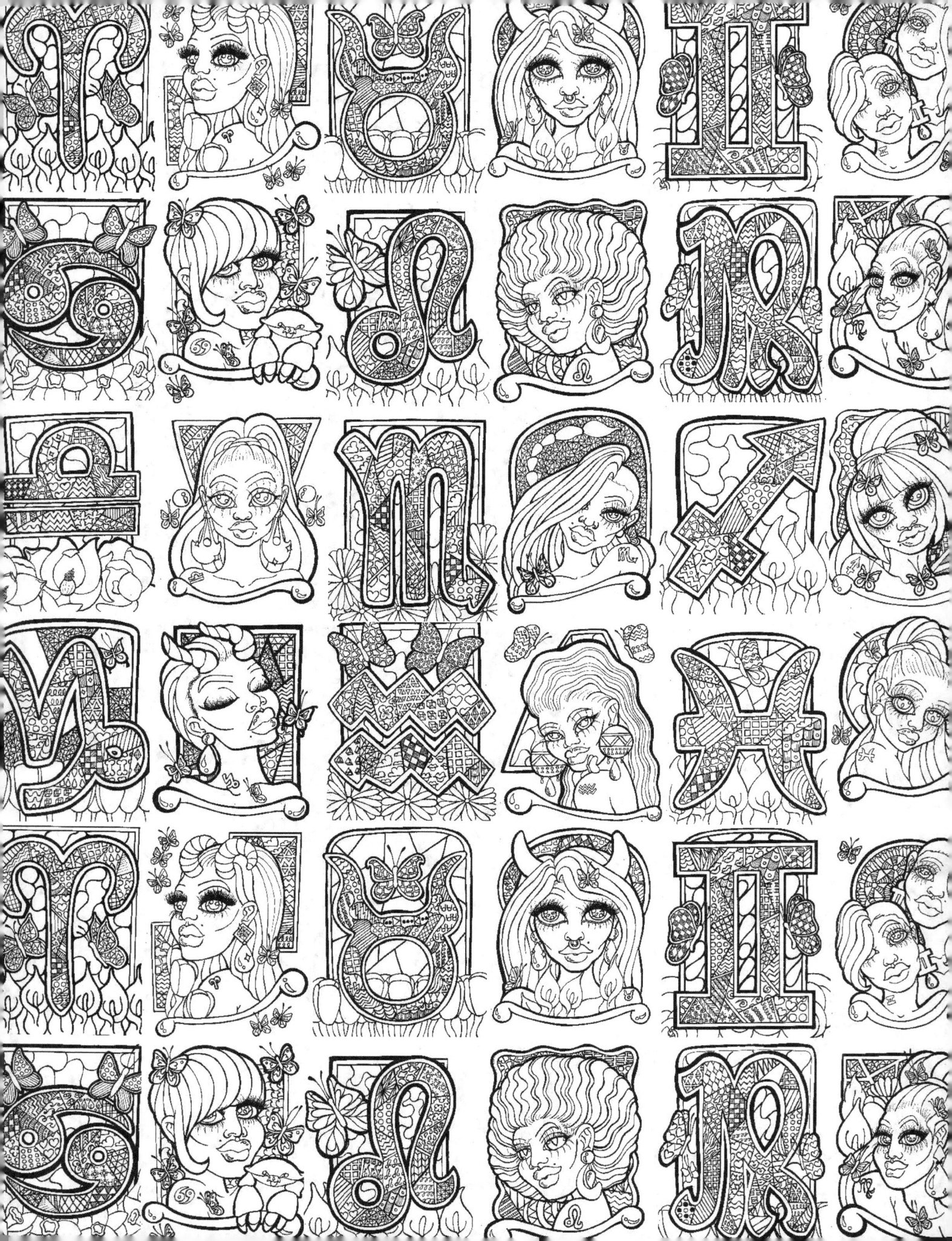

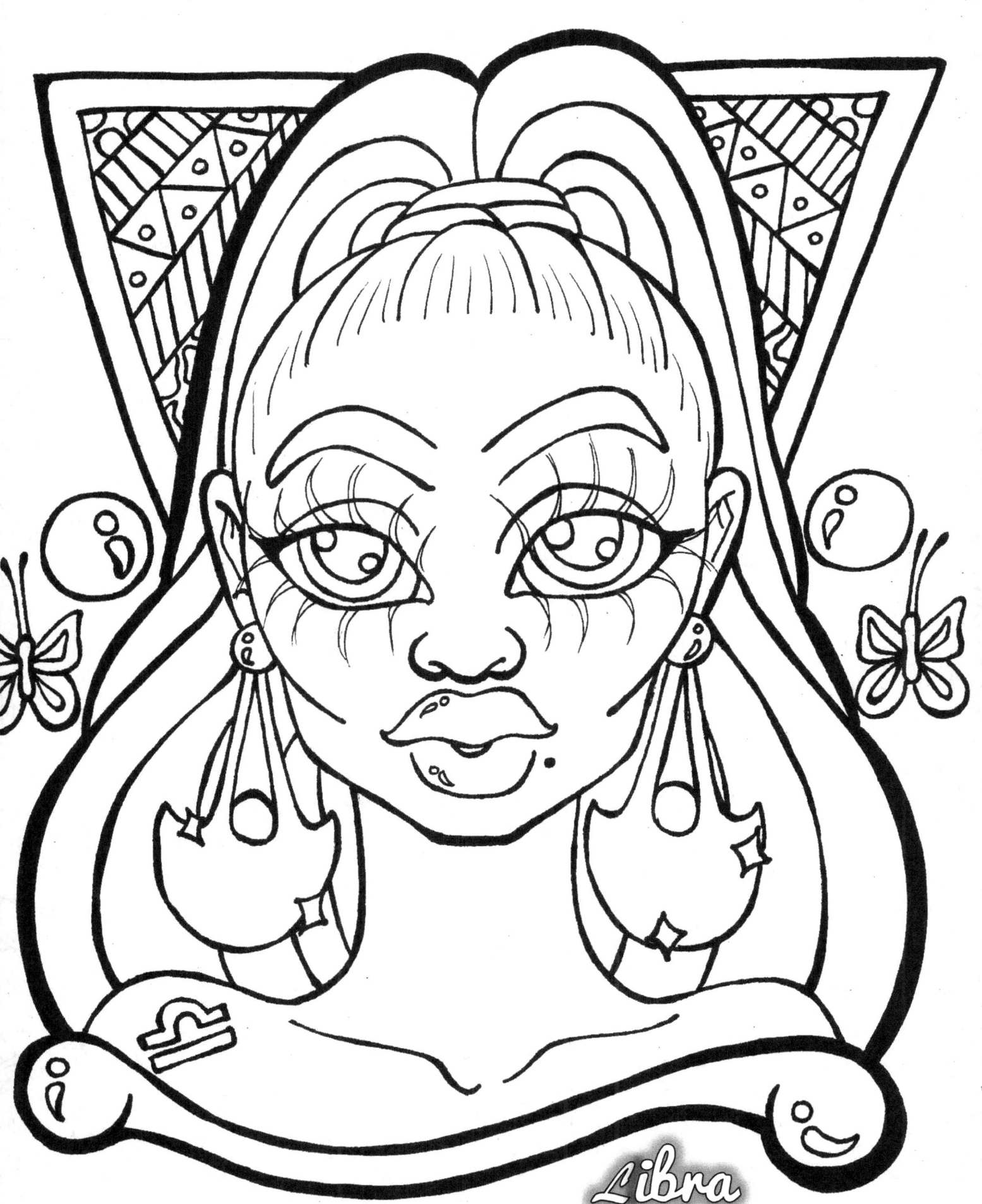

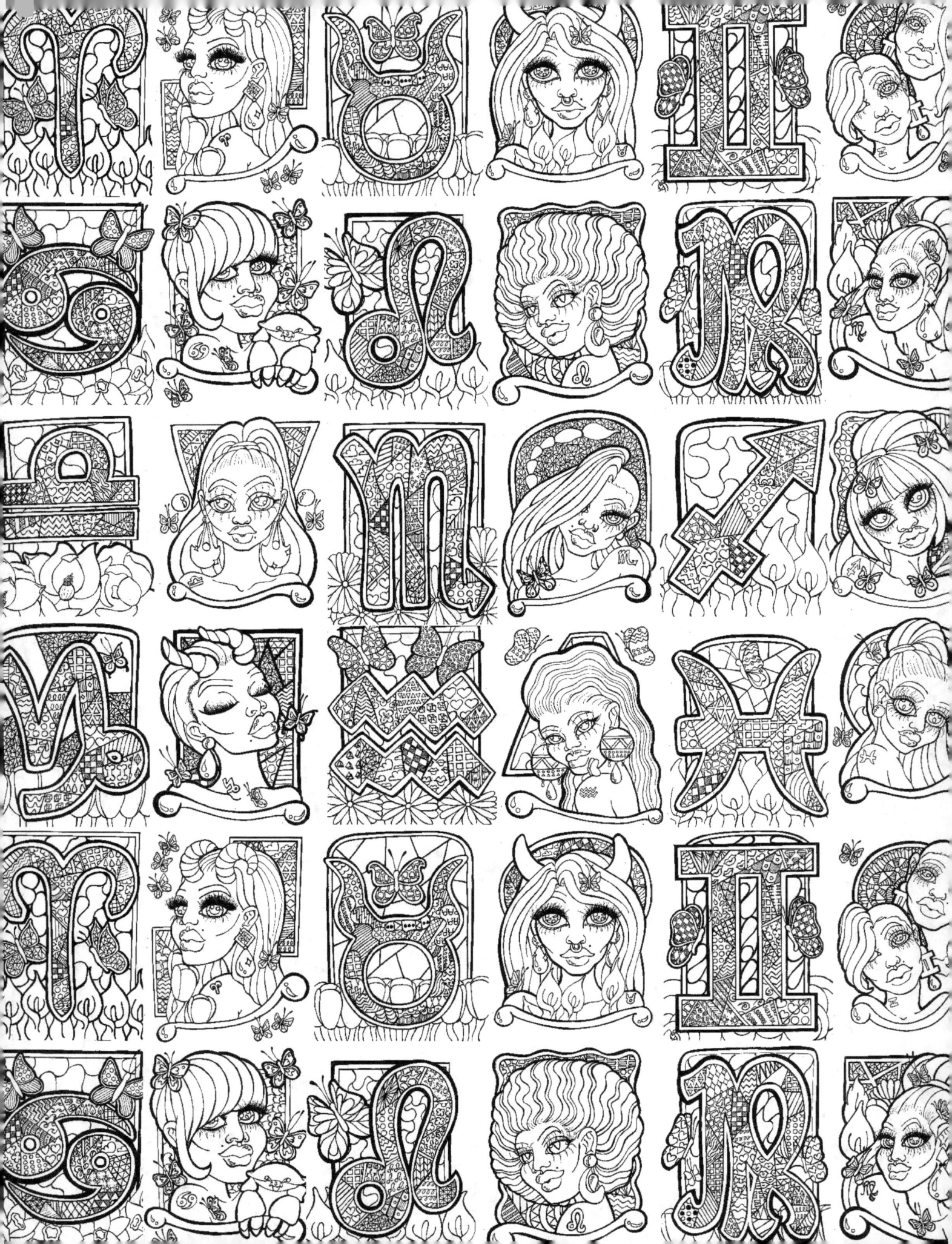

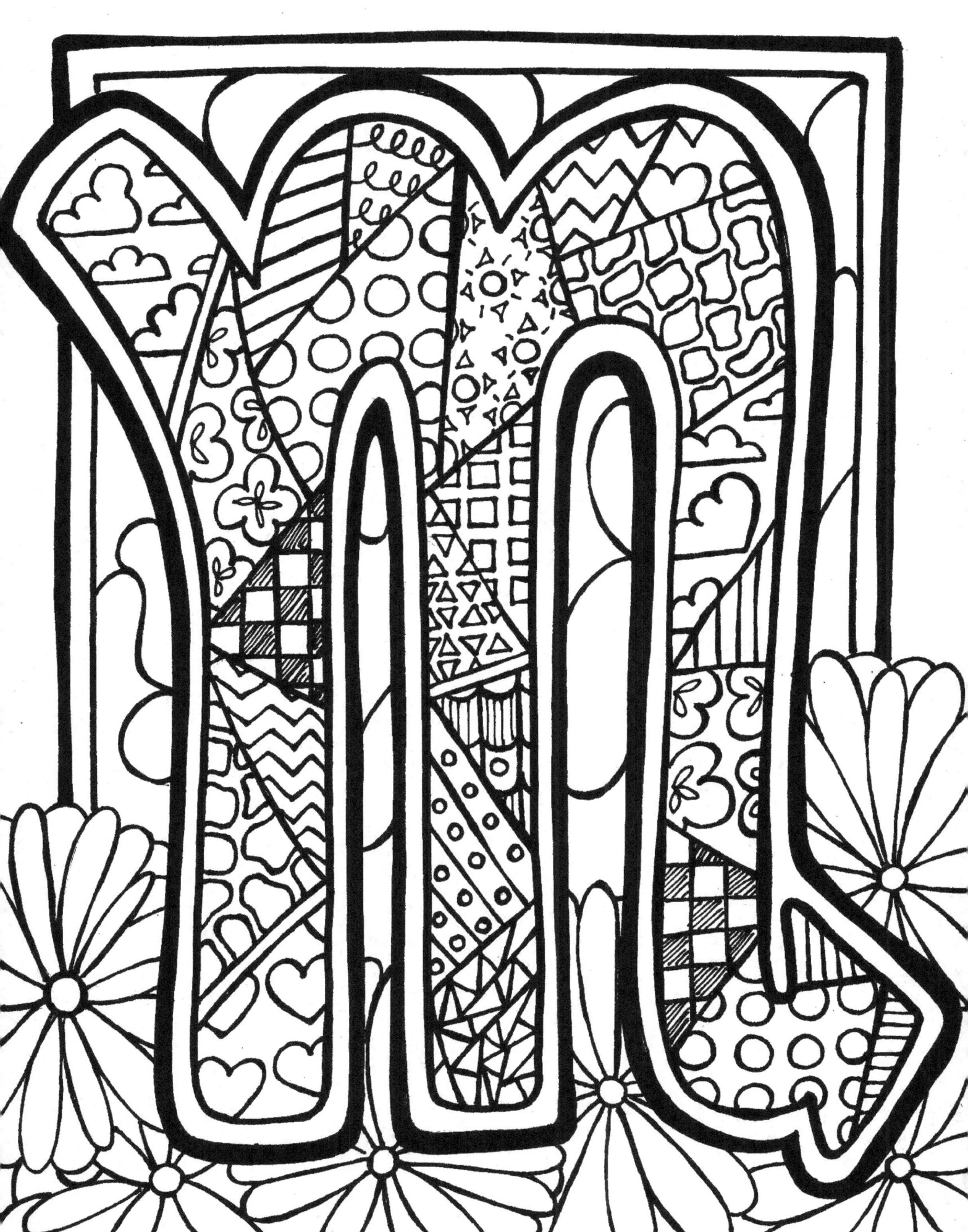

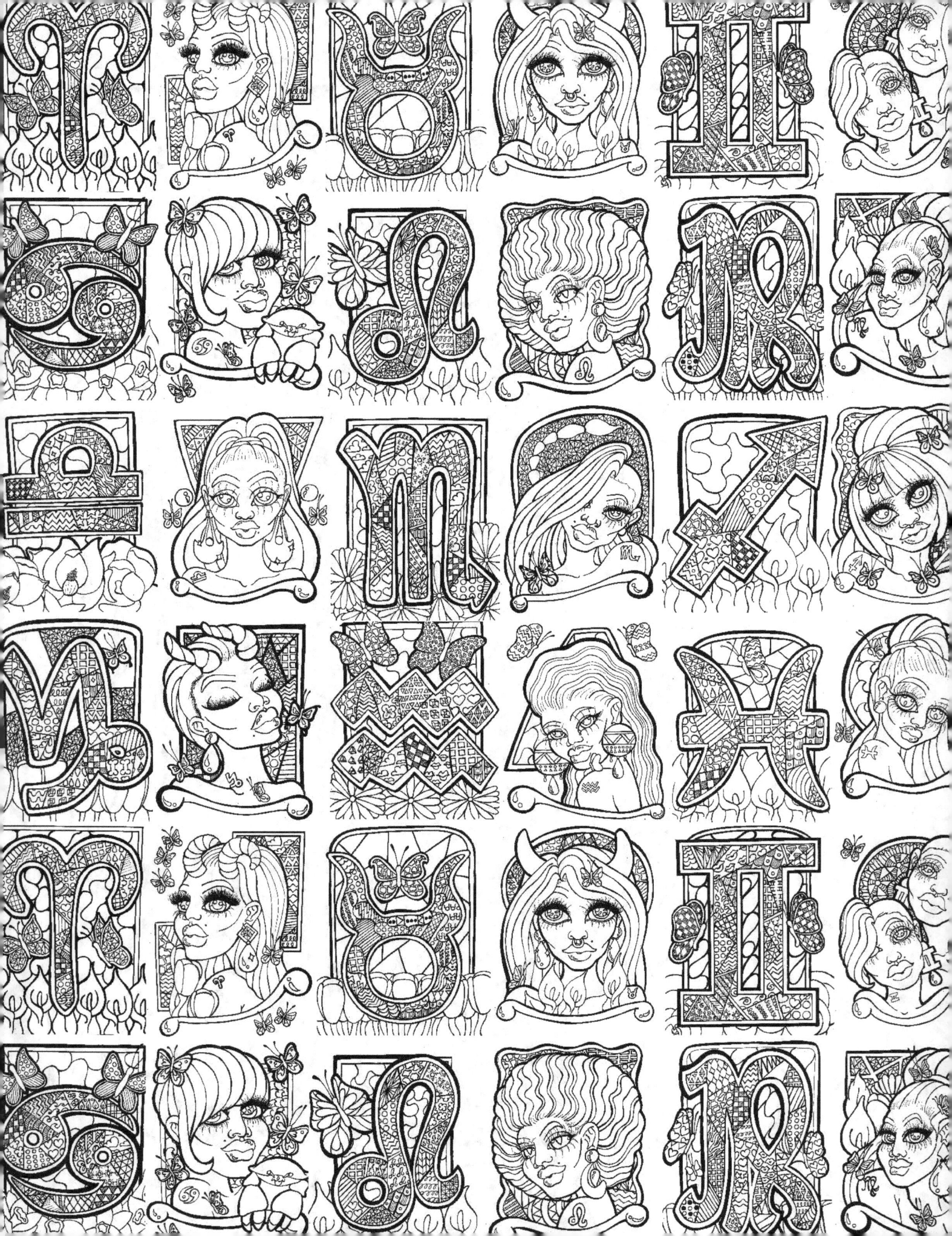

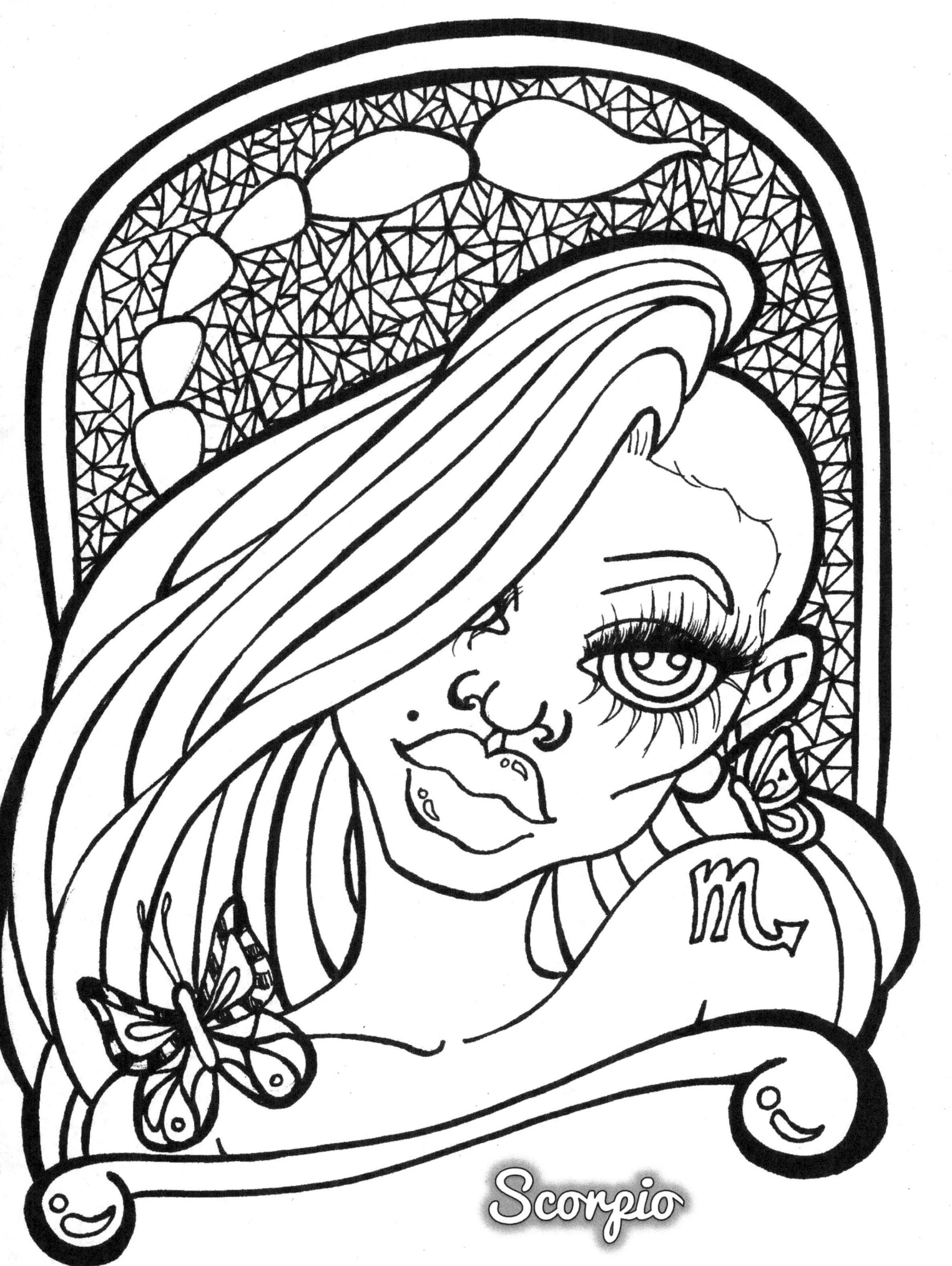

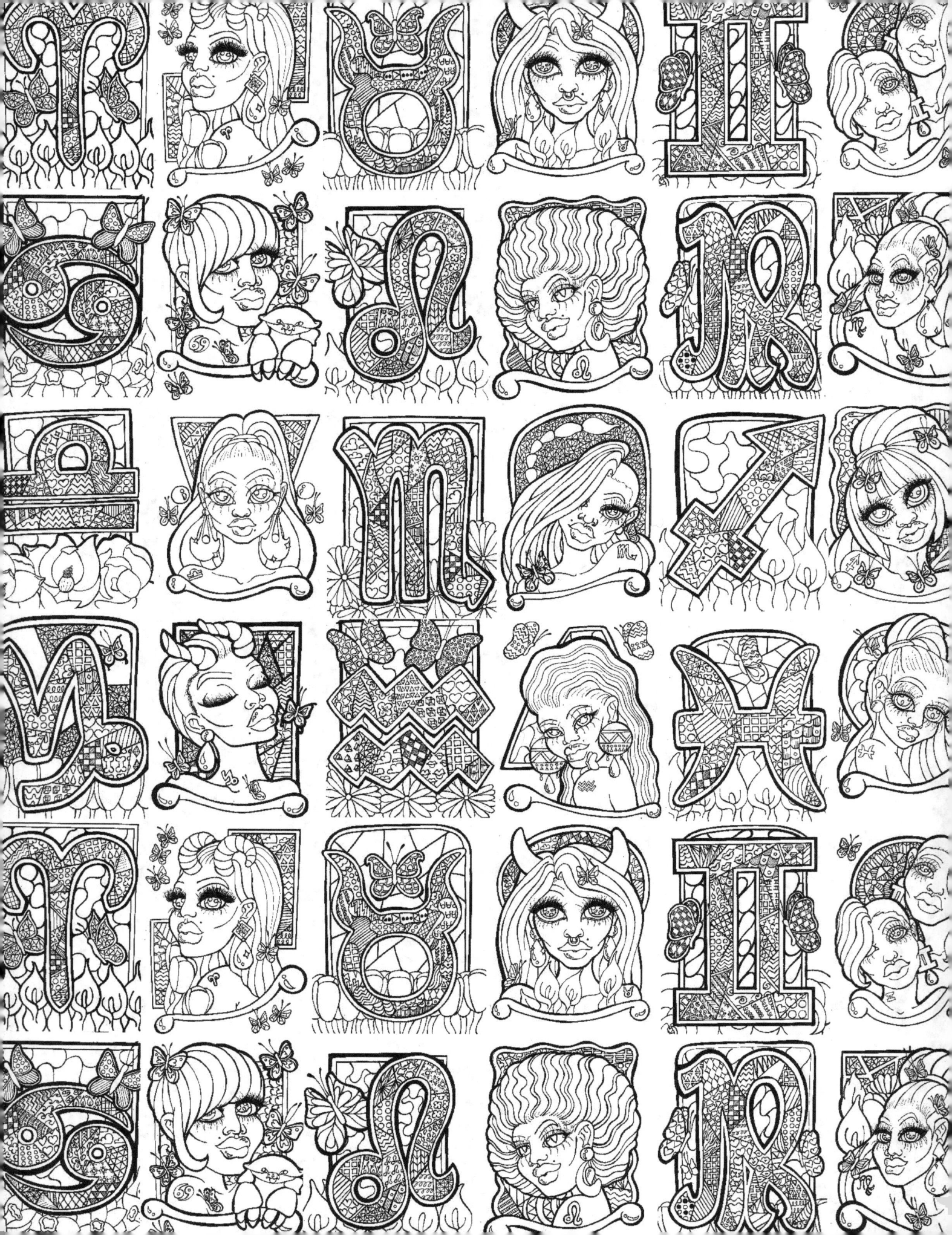

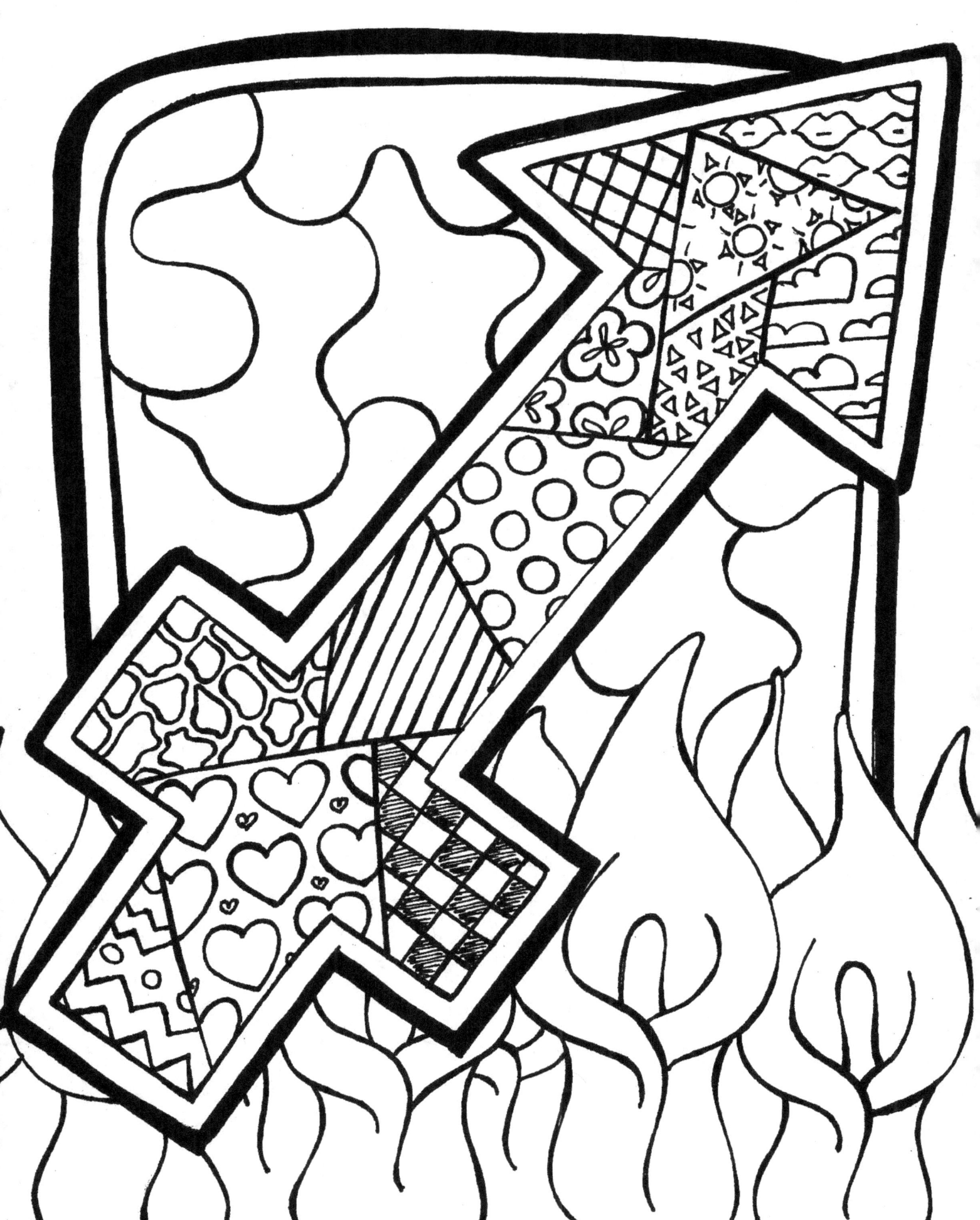

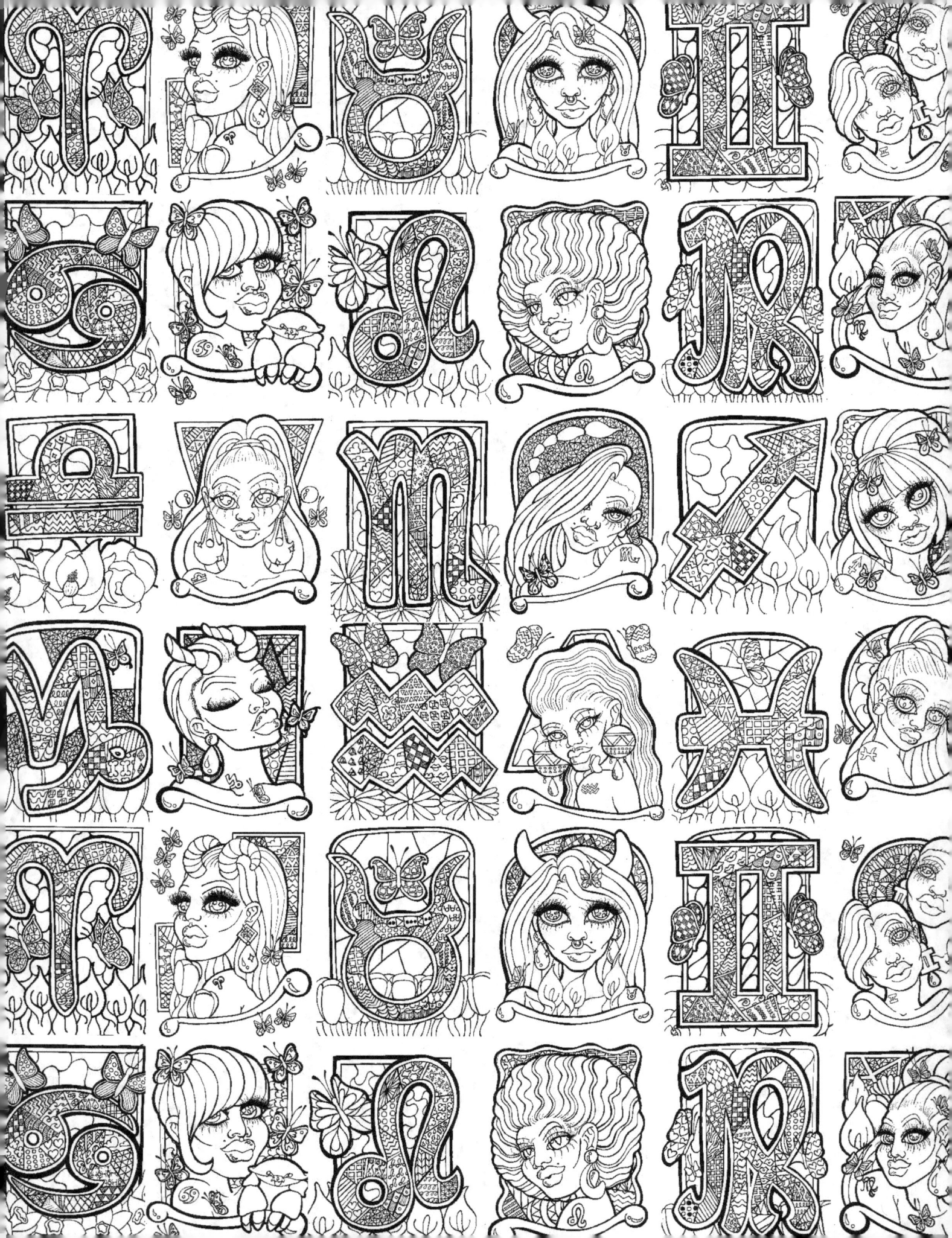

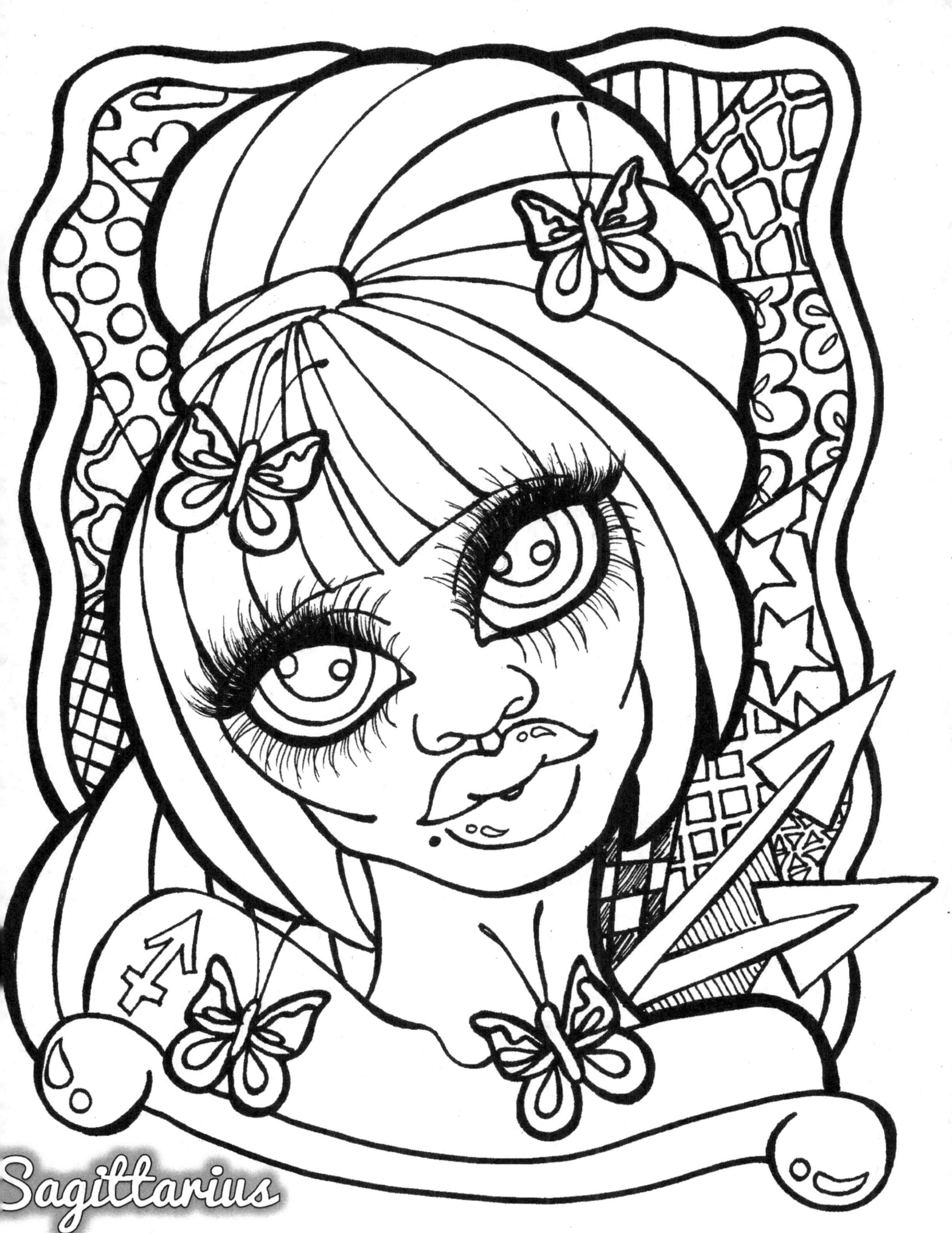

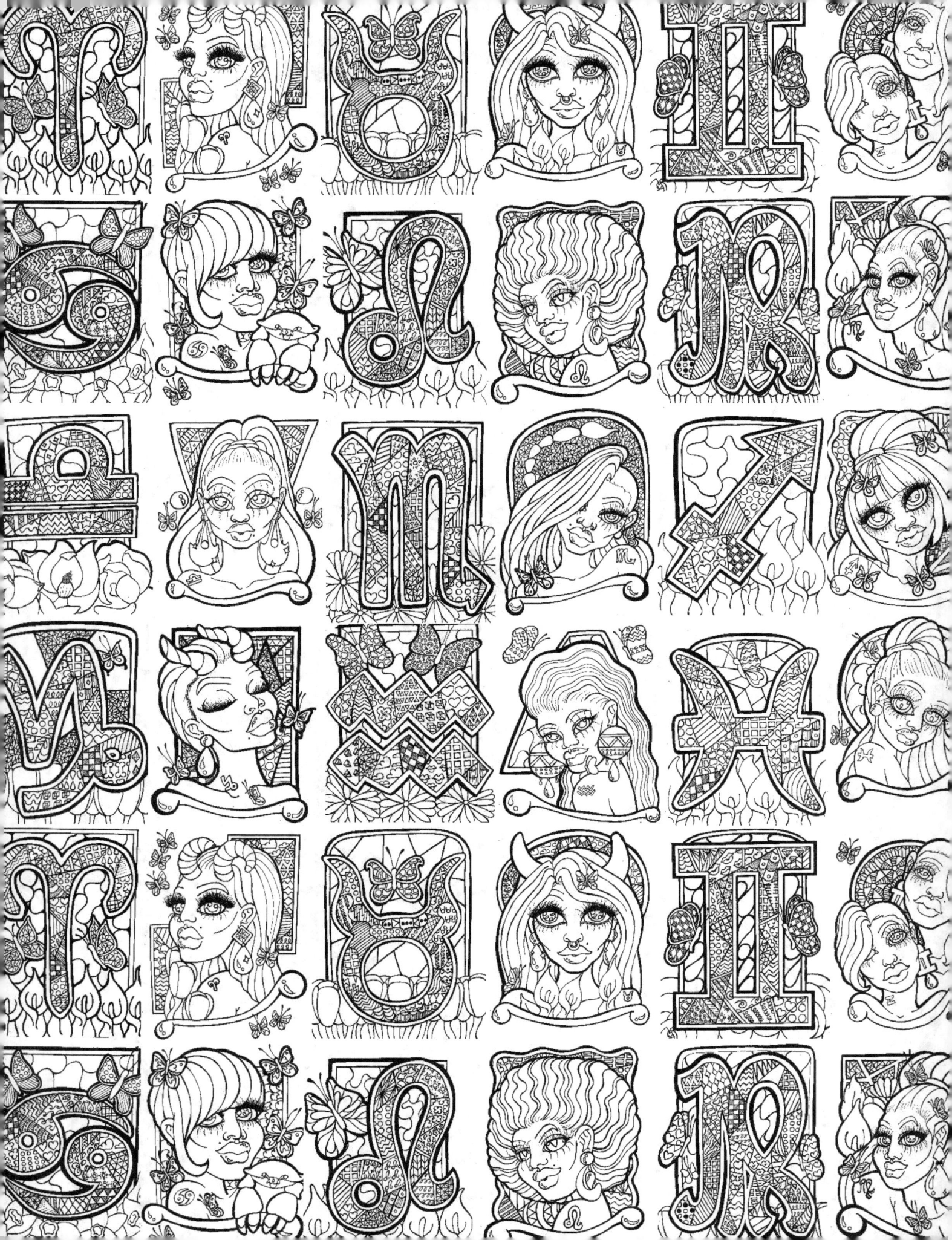

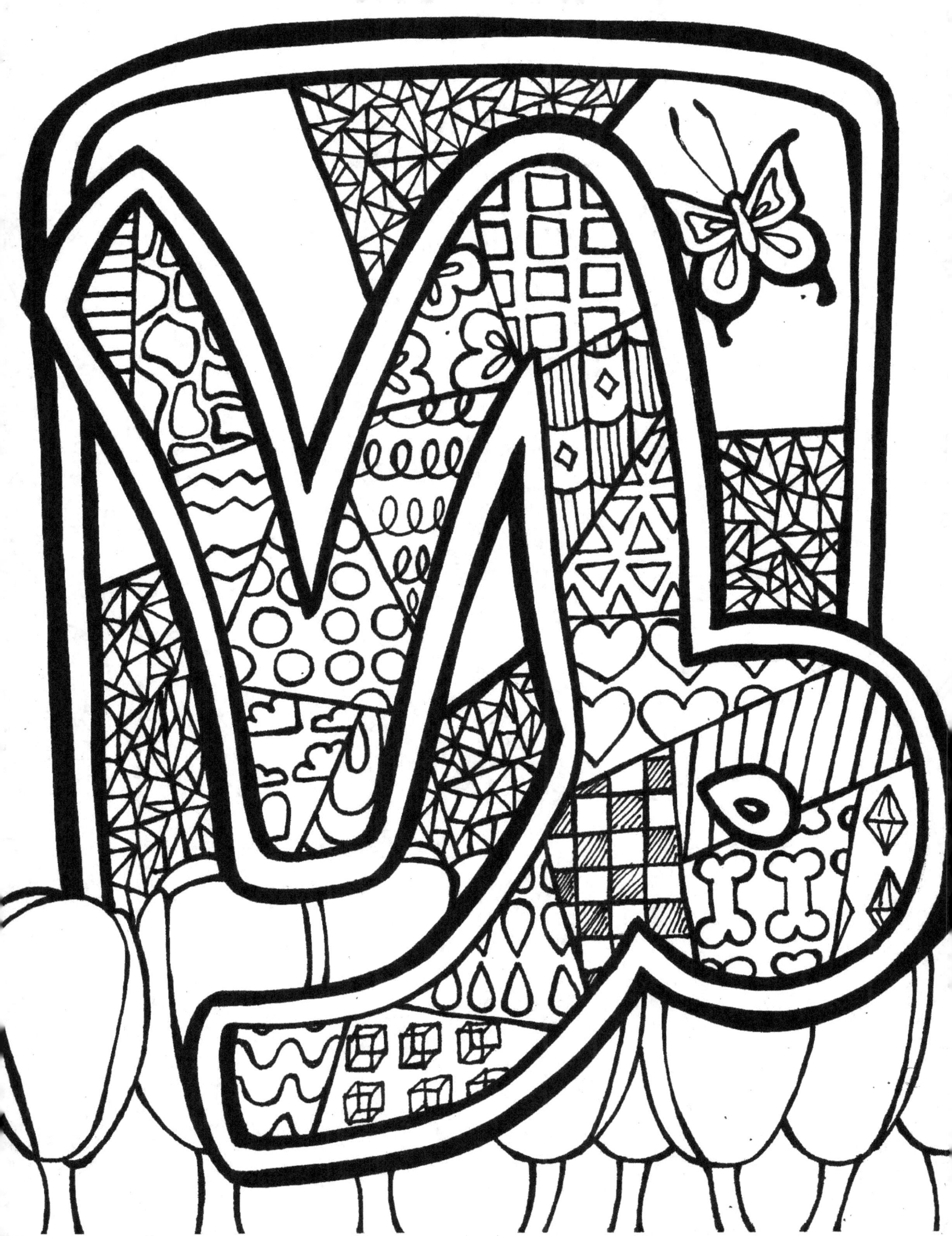

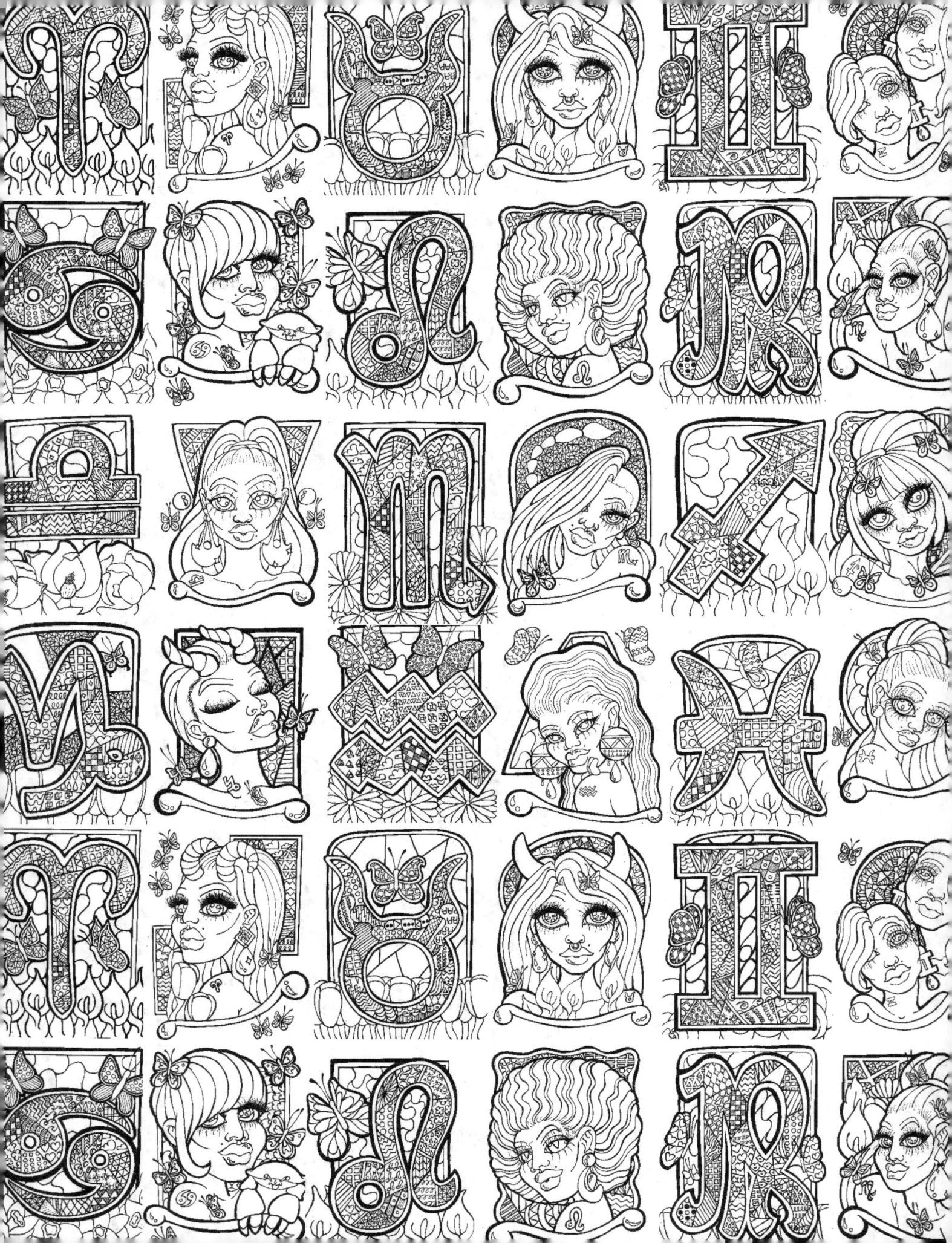

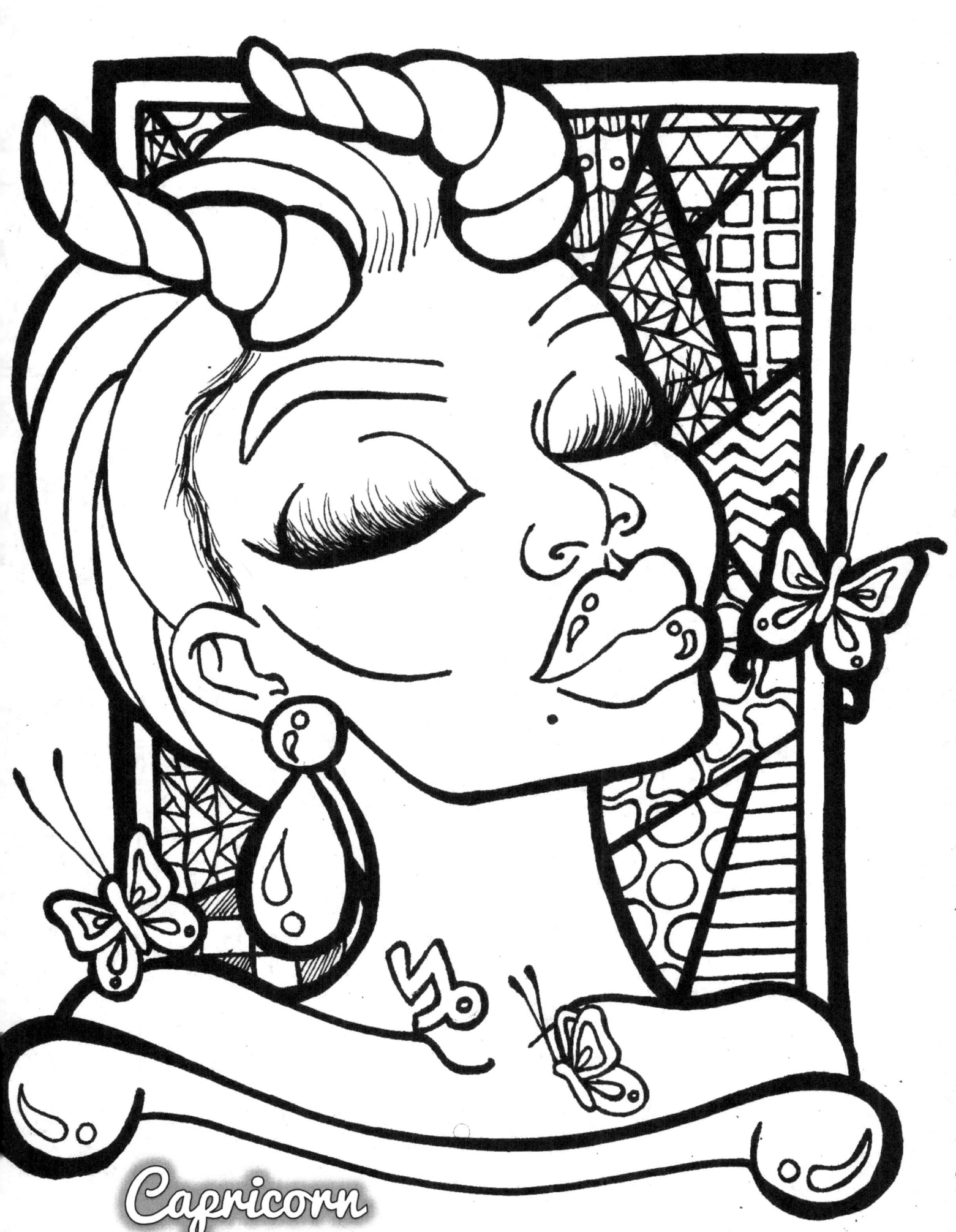

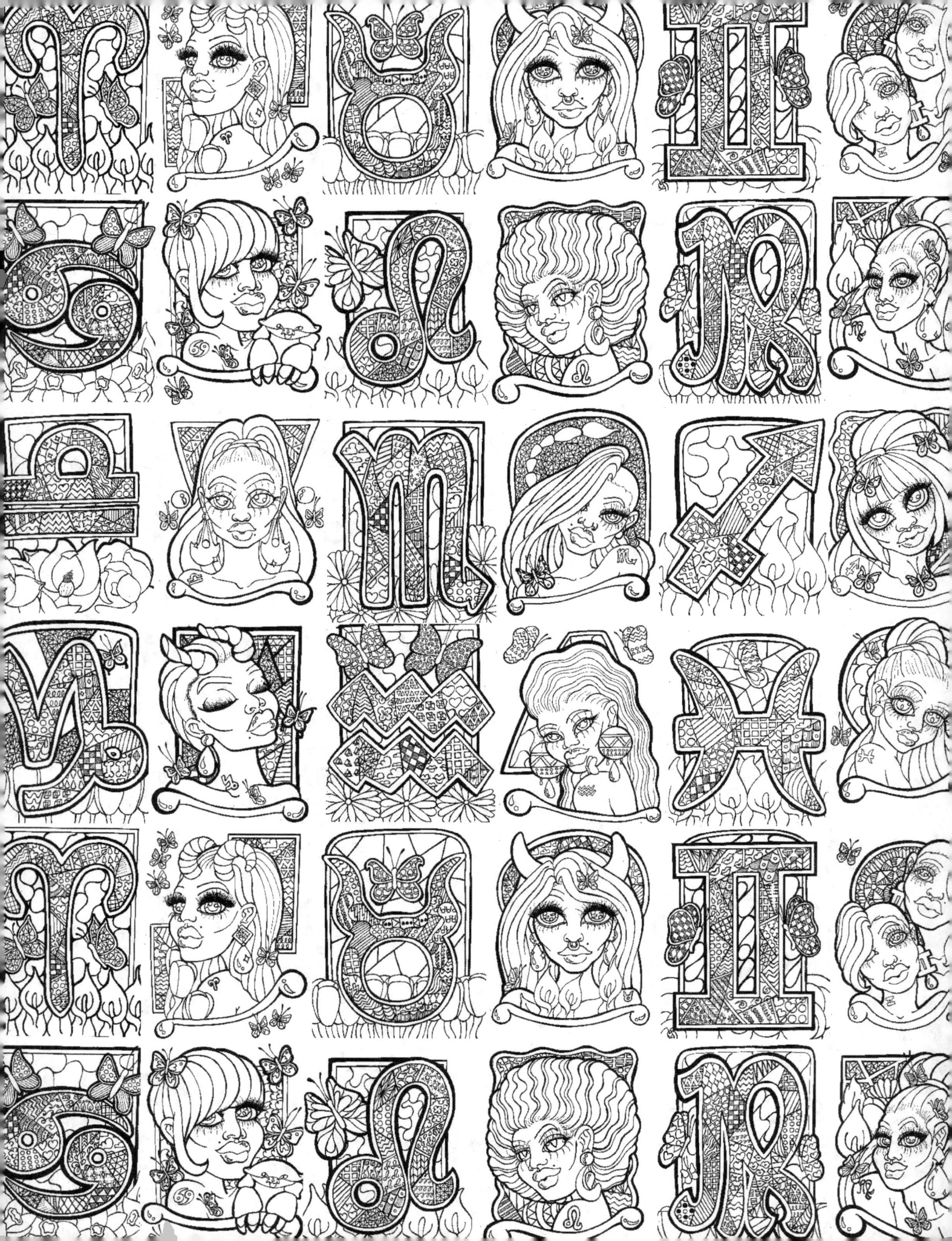

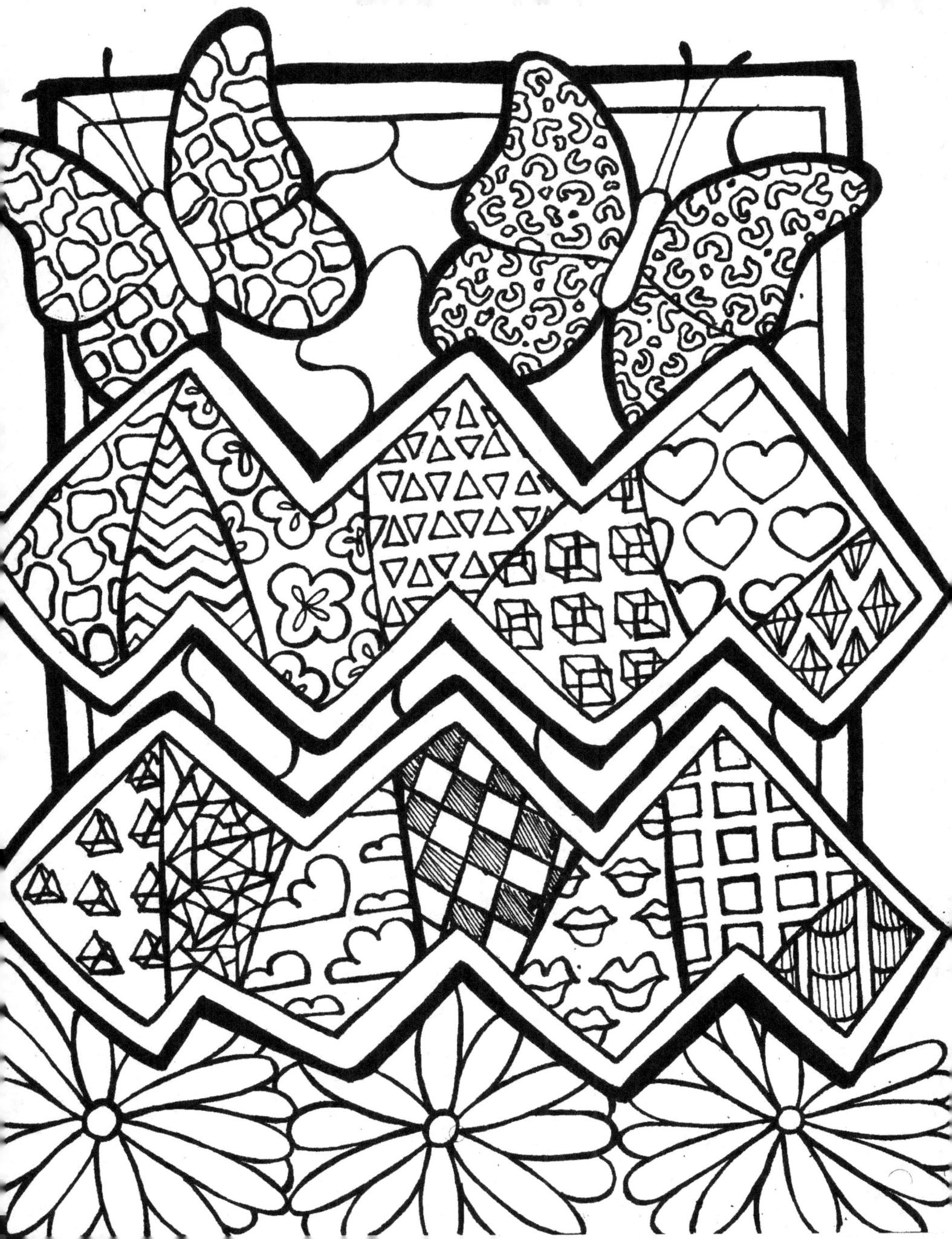

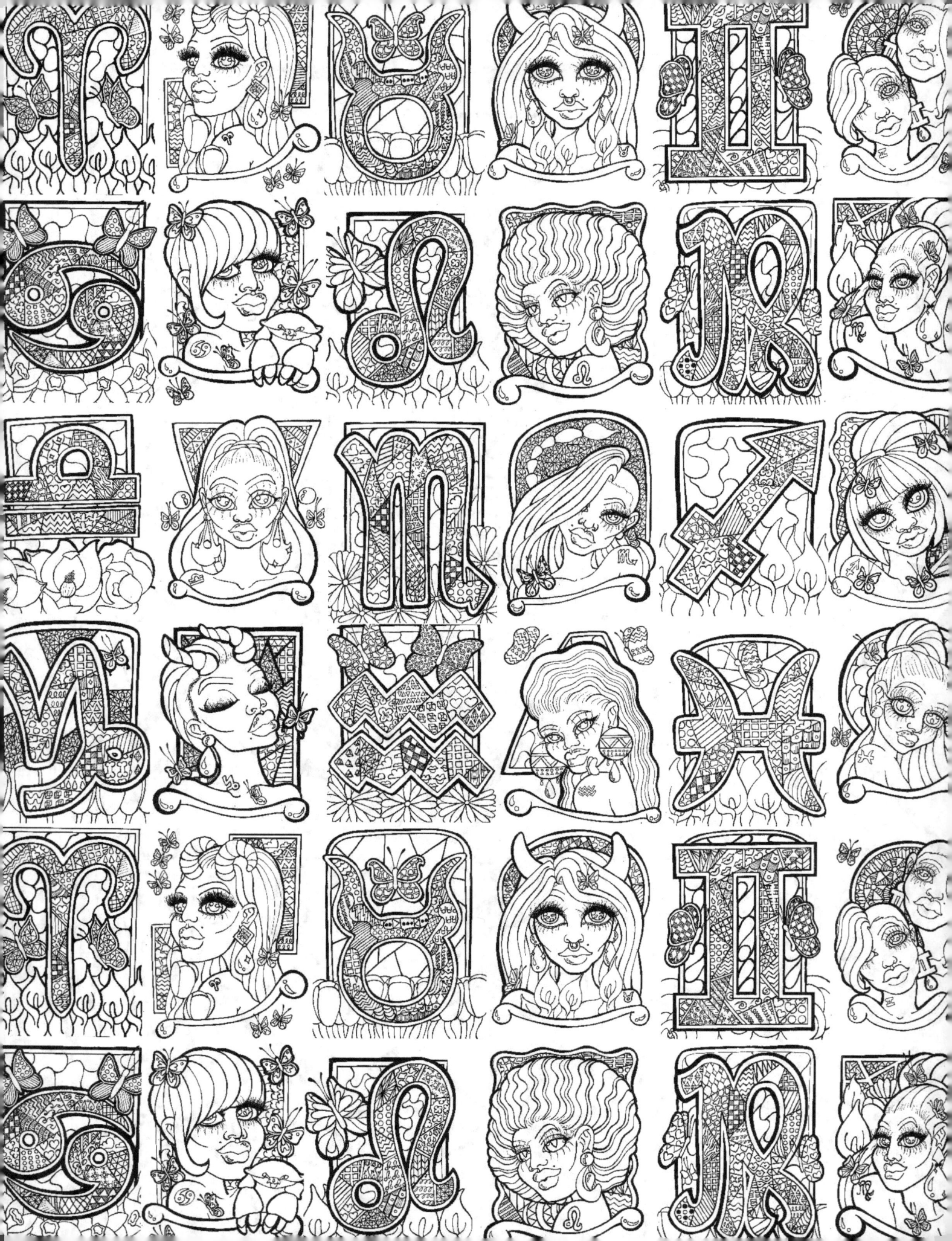

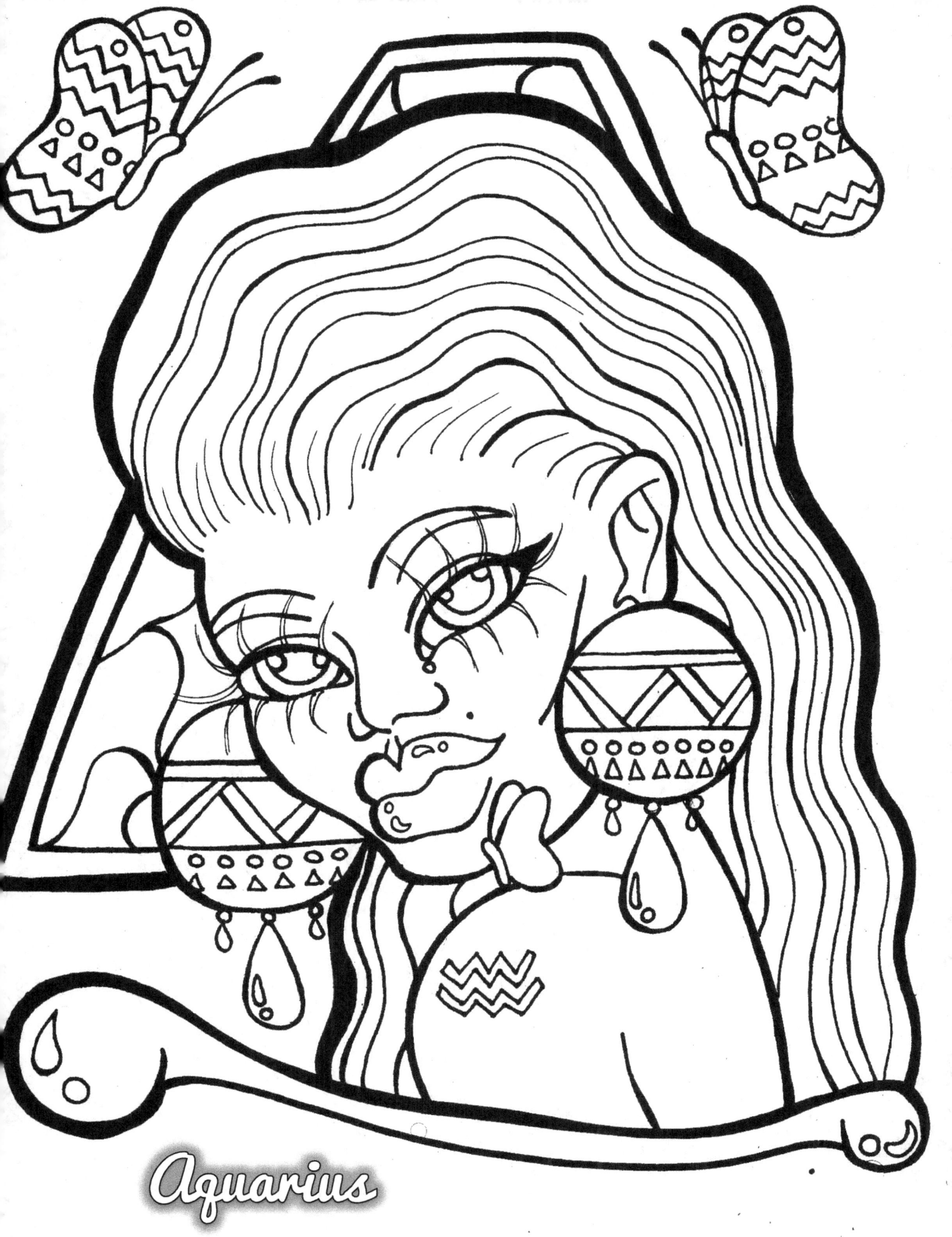

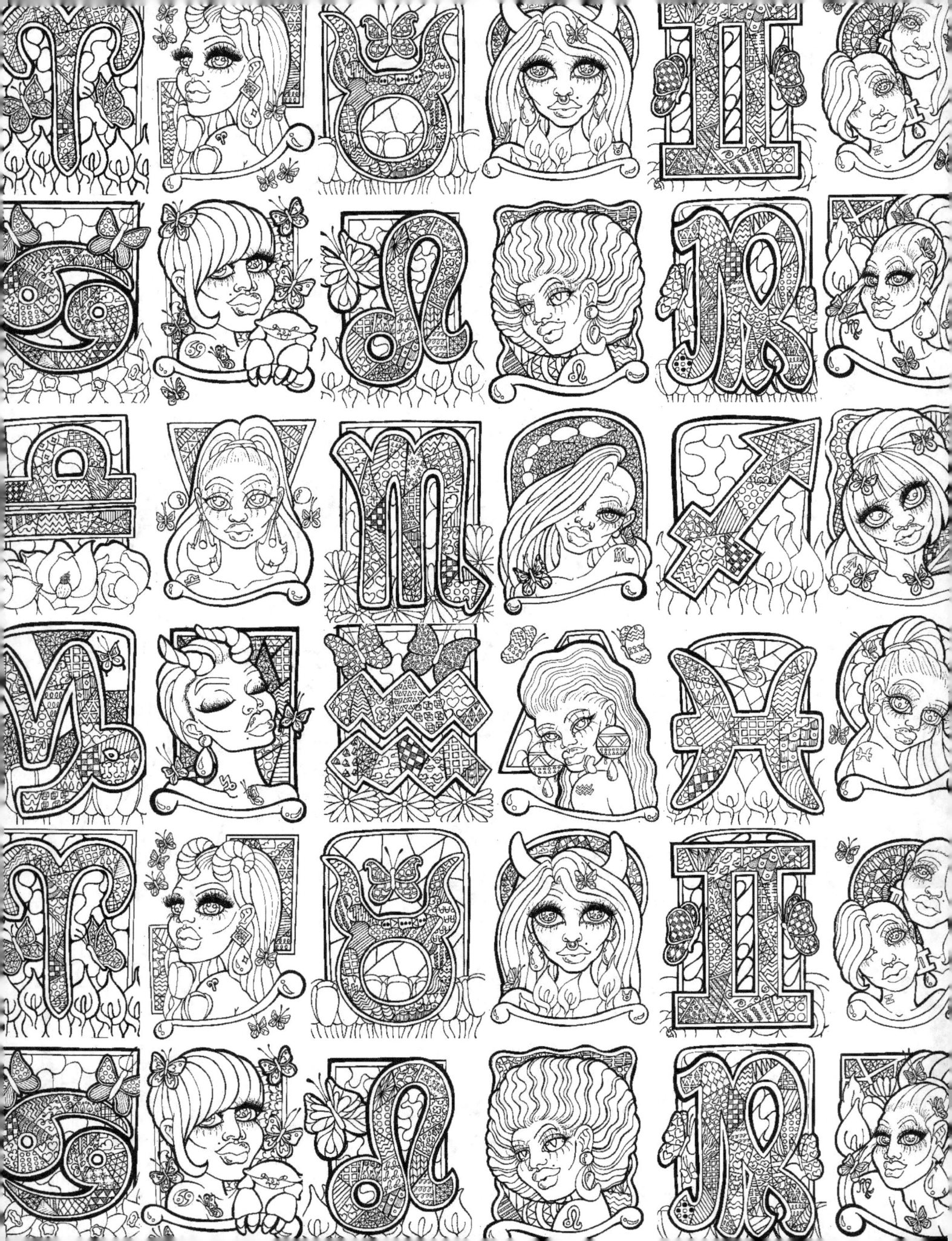

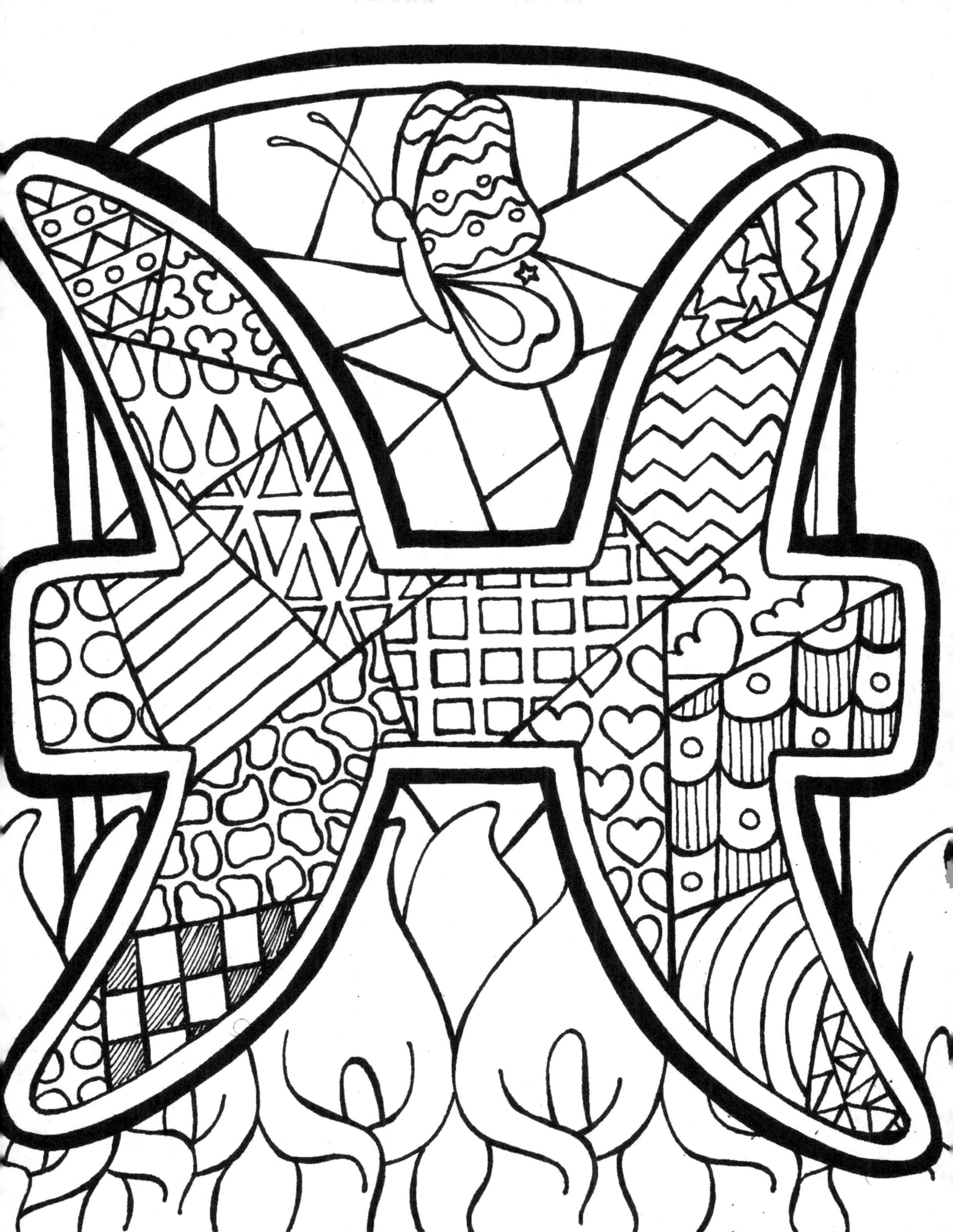

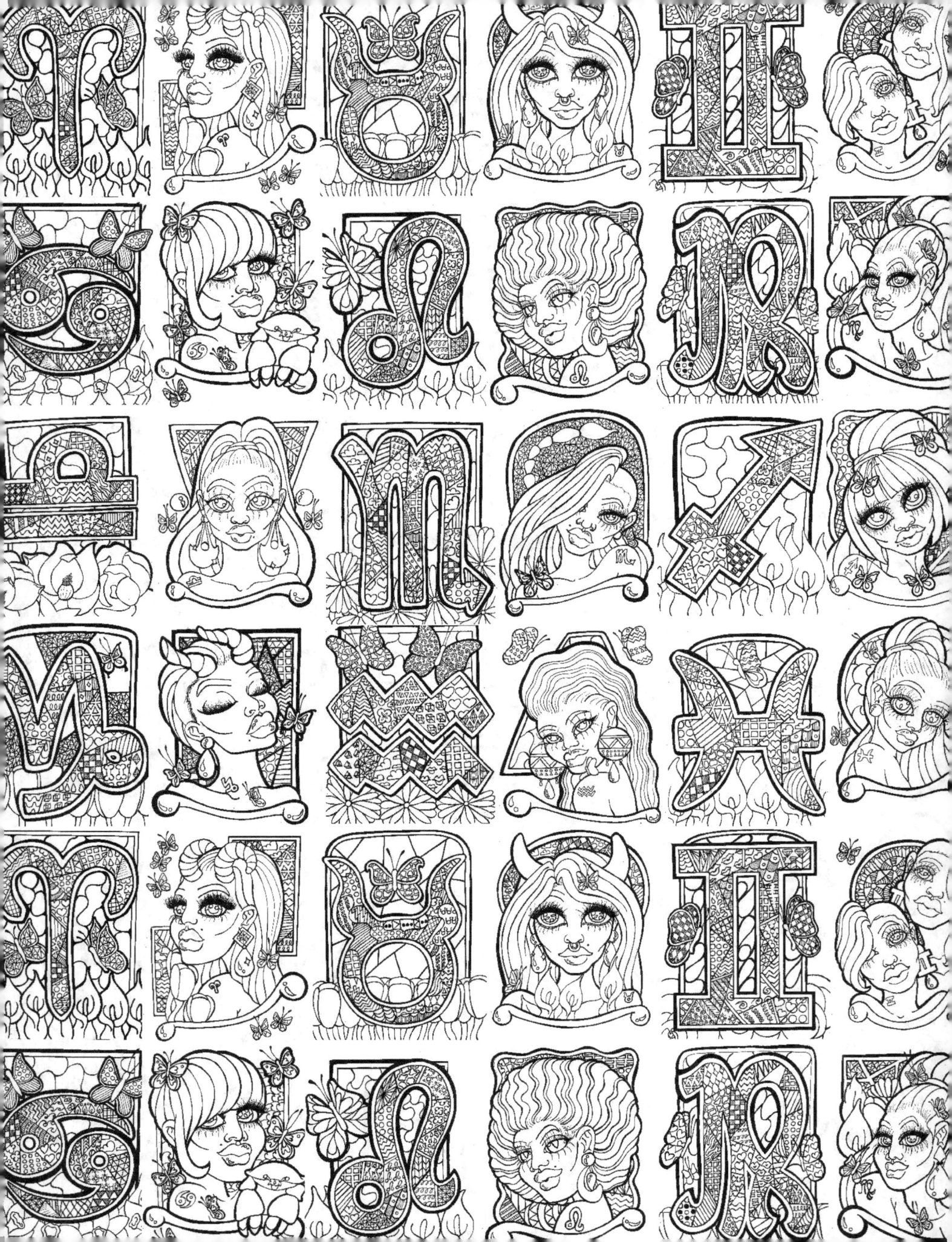

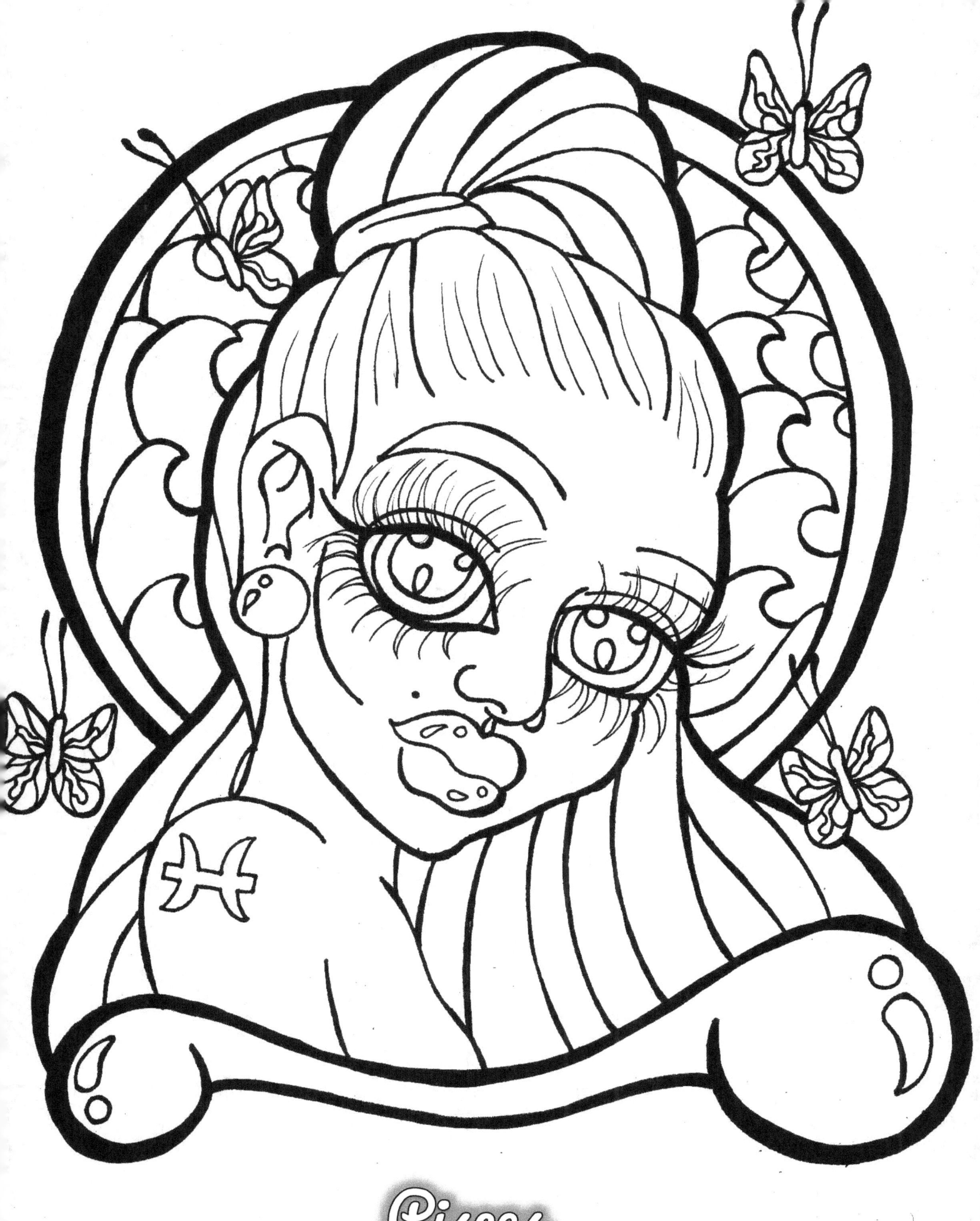

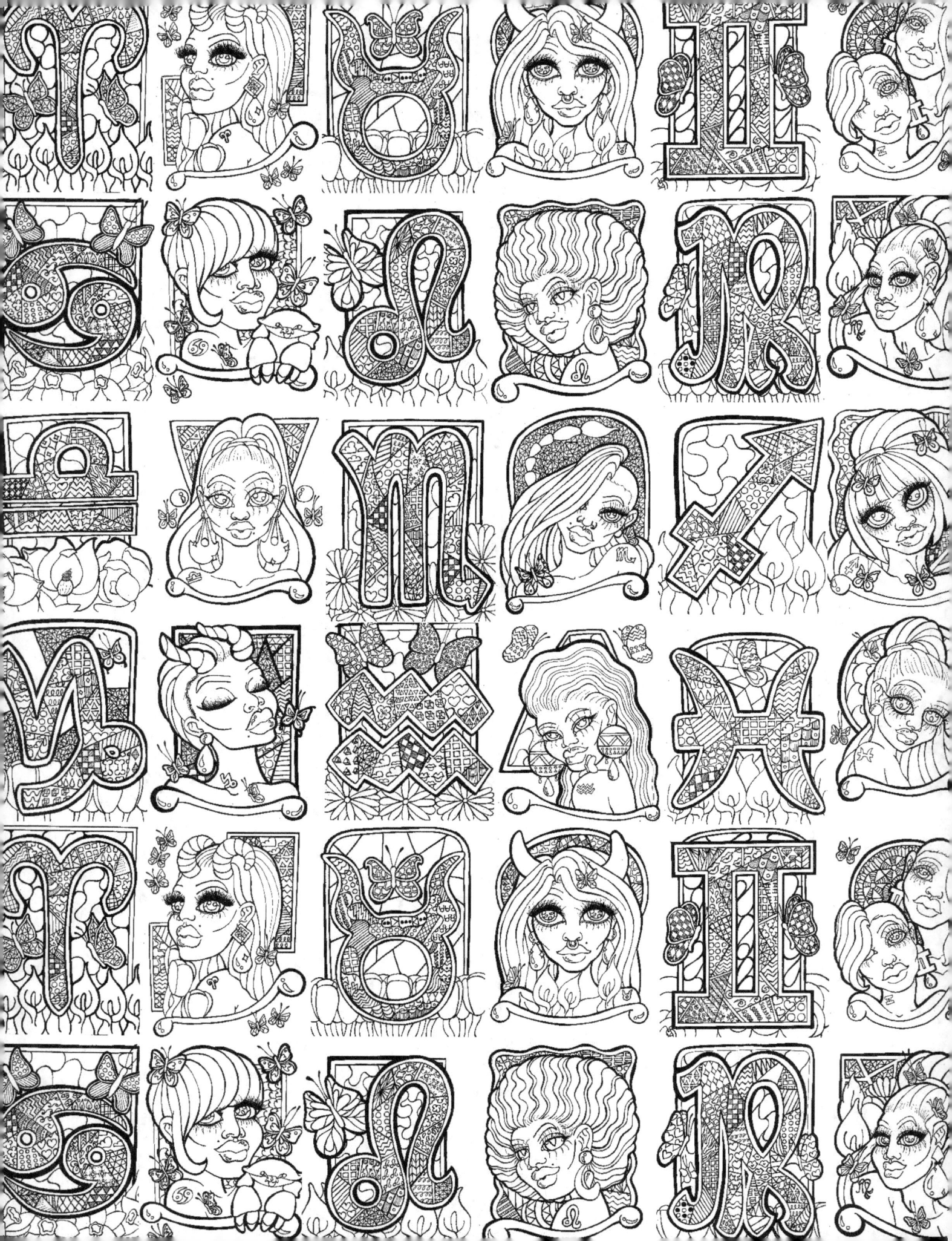

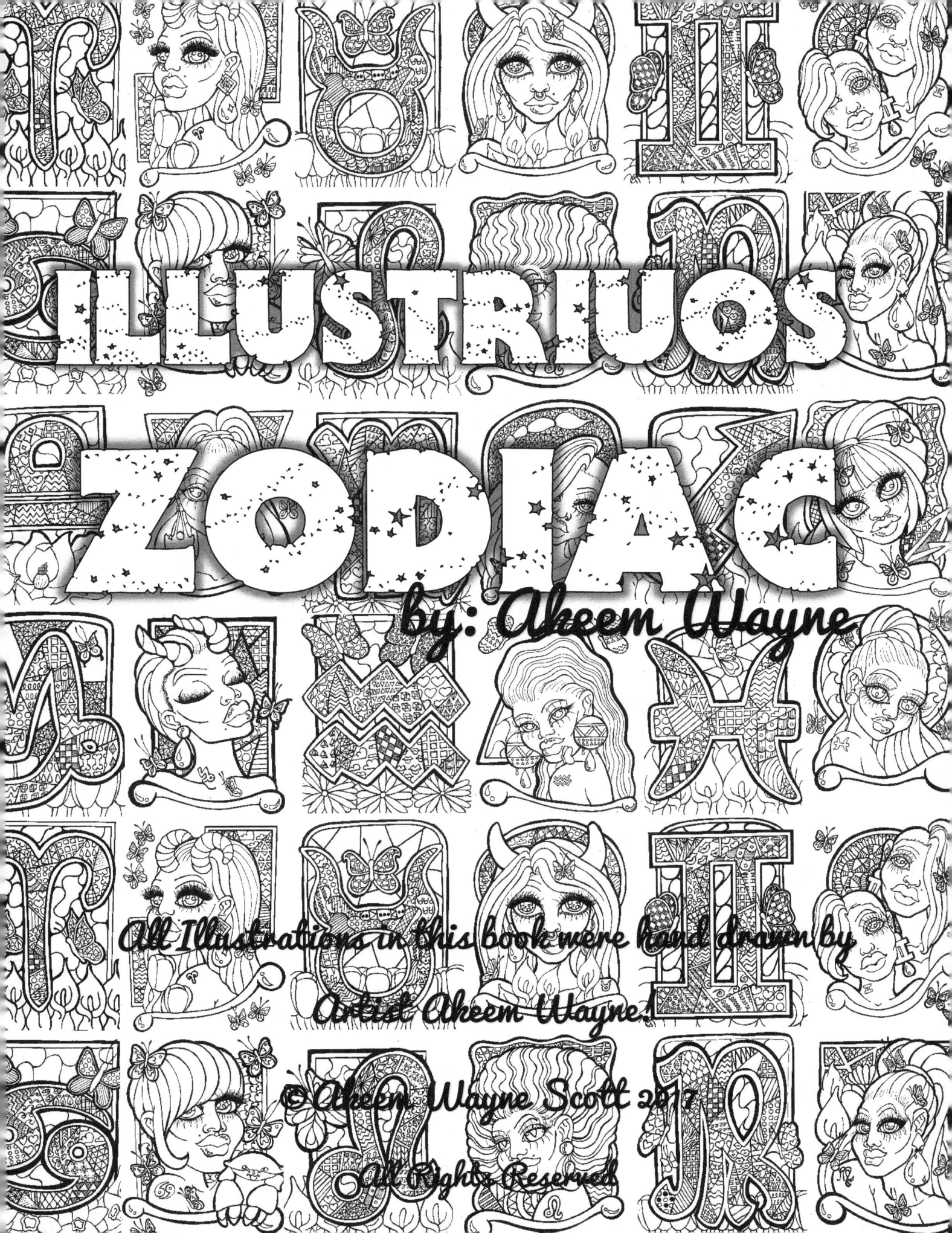

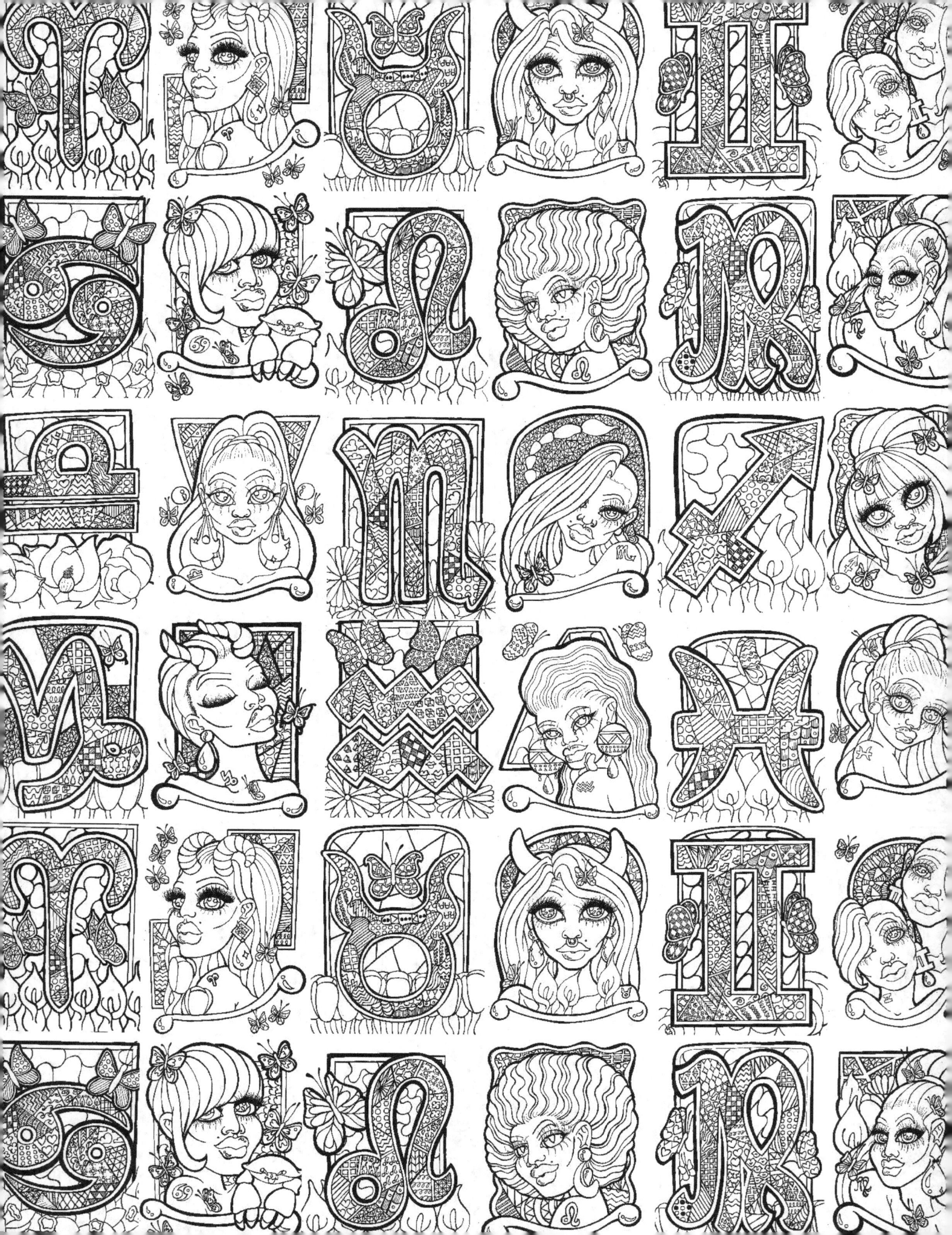

Thank you for adding Illustrious Zodiac to your Coloring Book Collection. Please check out other books in the Illustrious Coloring Book Collection!

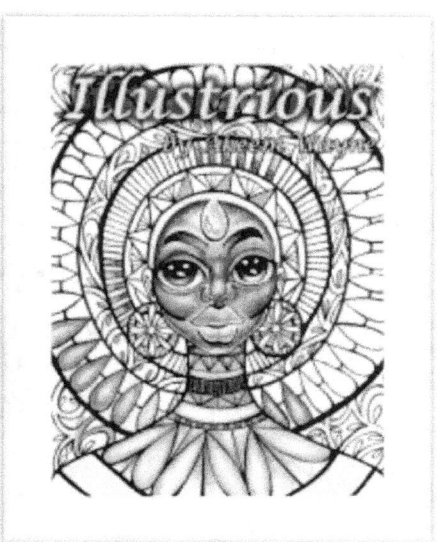
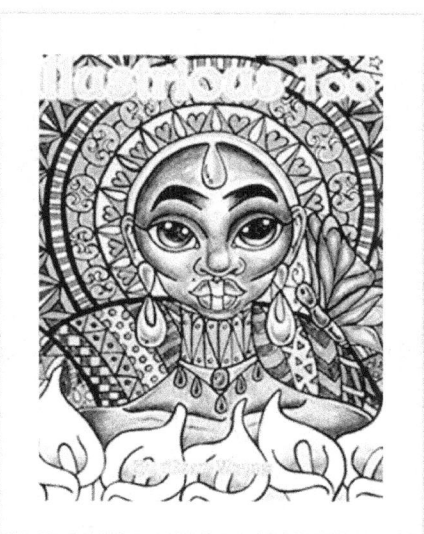
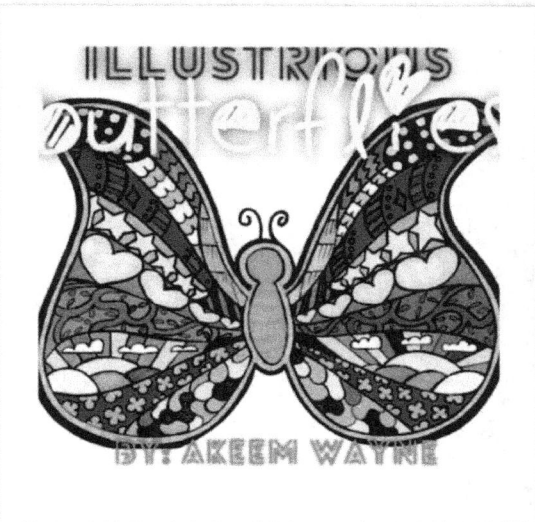

Available on :

www.akeemwayne.com

&

www.etsy.com

Social Media:

FB: The Art of Akeem - IG: @IllustriousColoringBooks

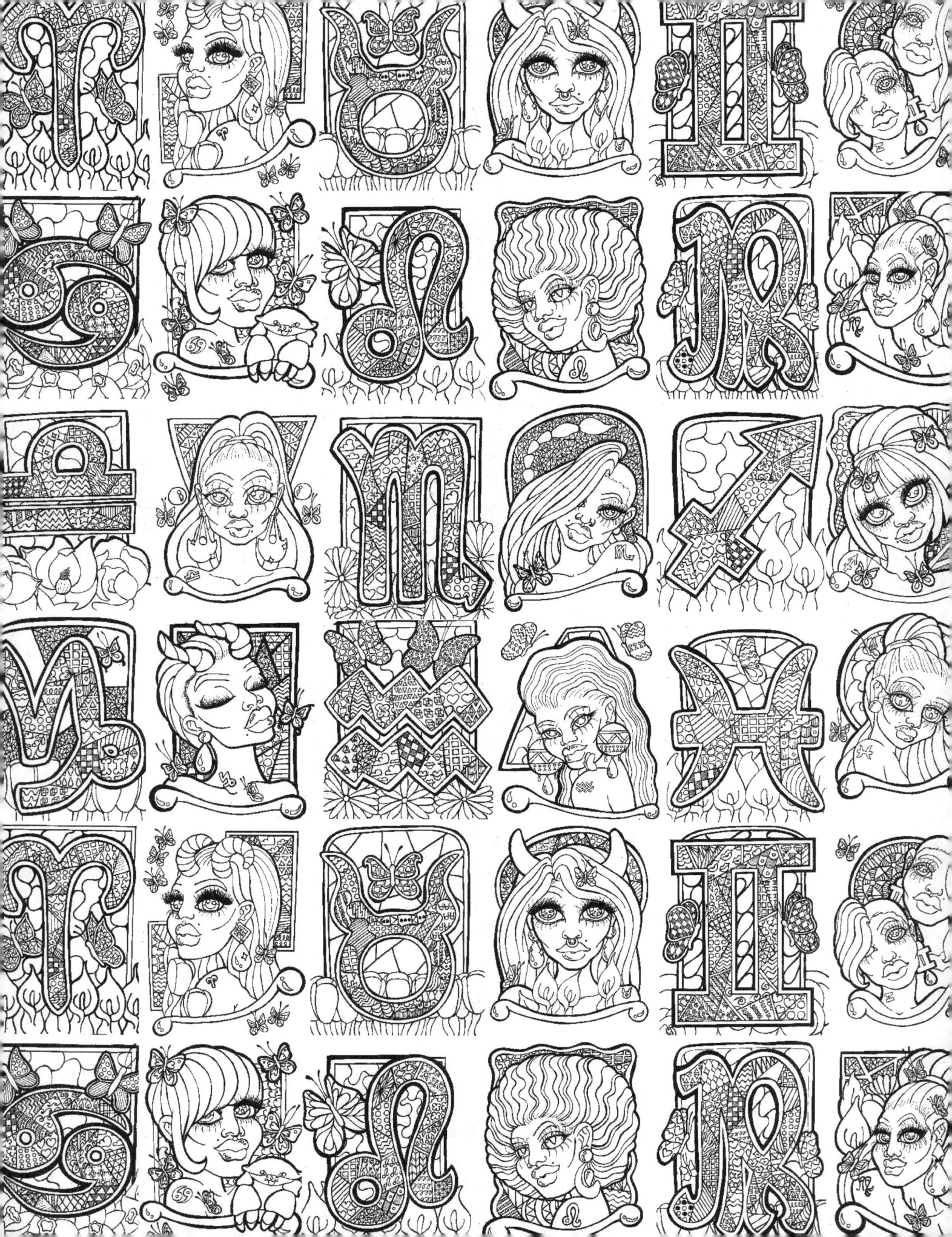

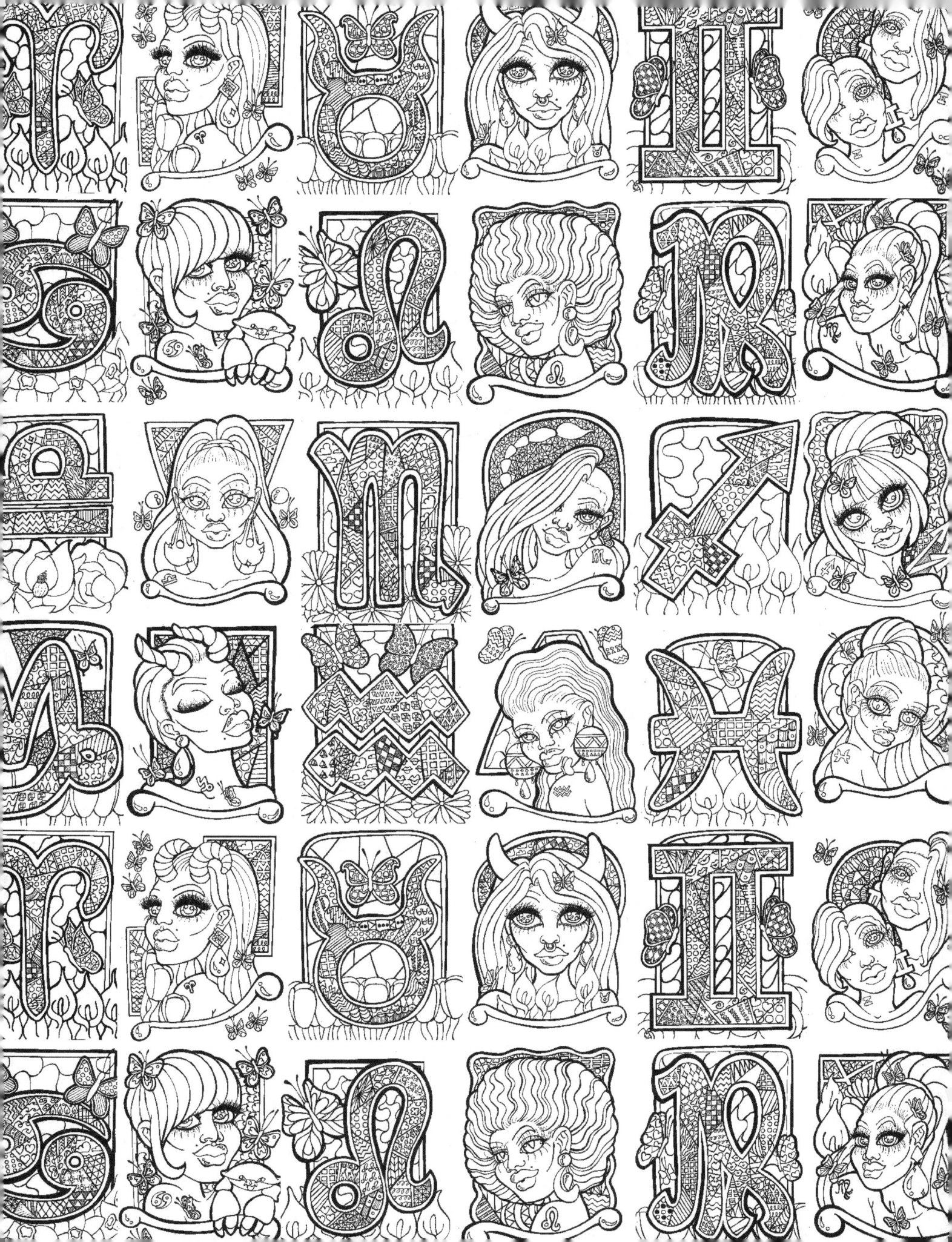

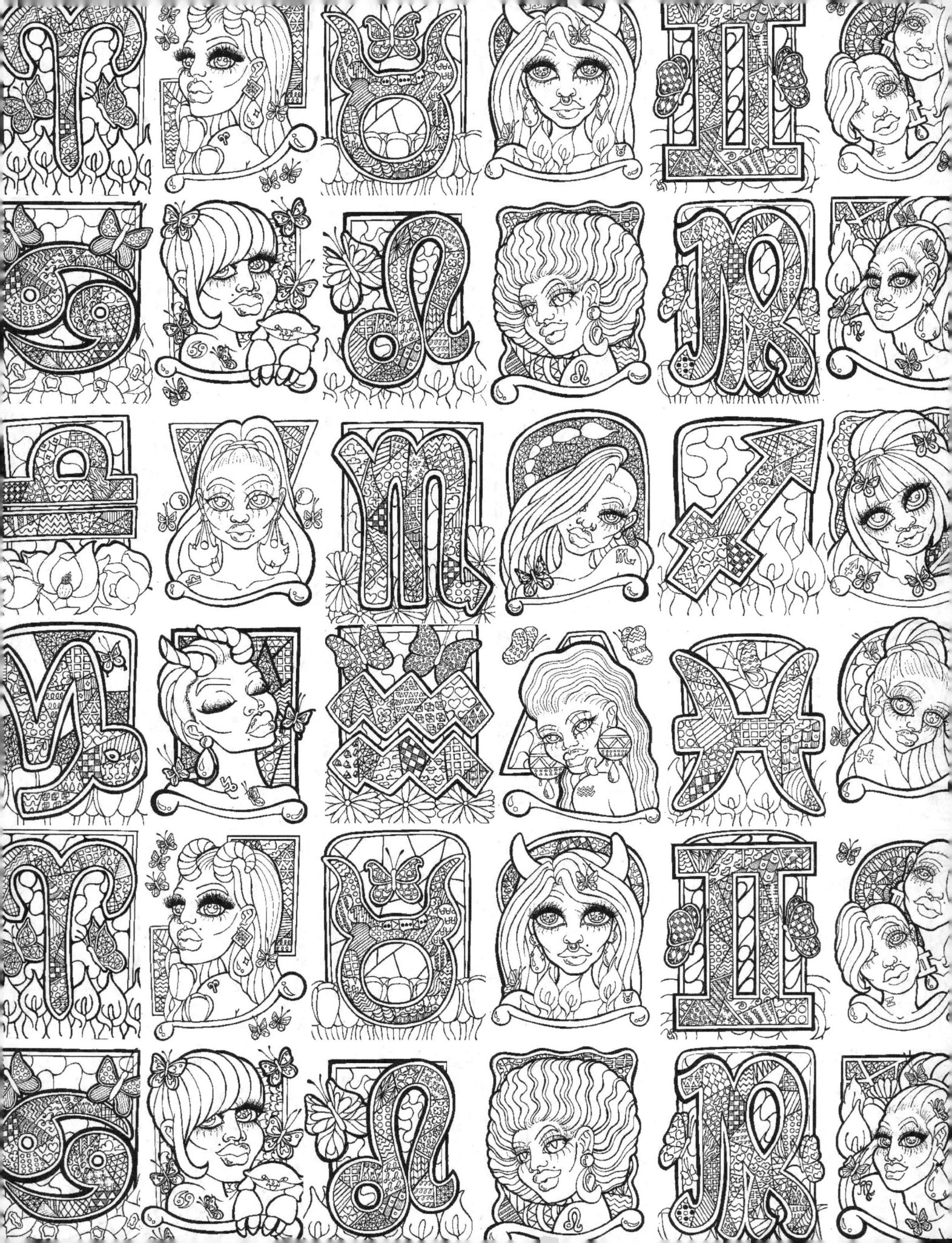

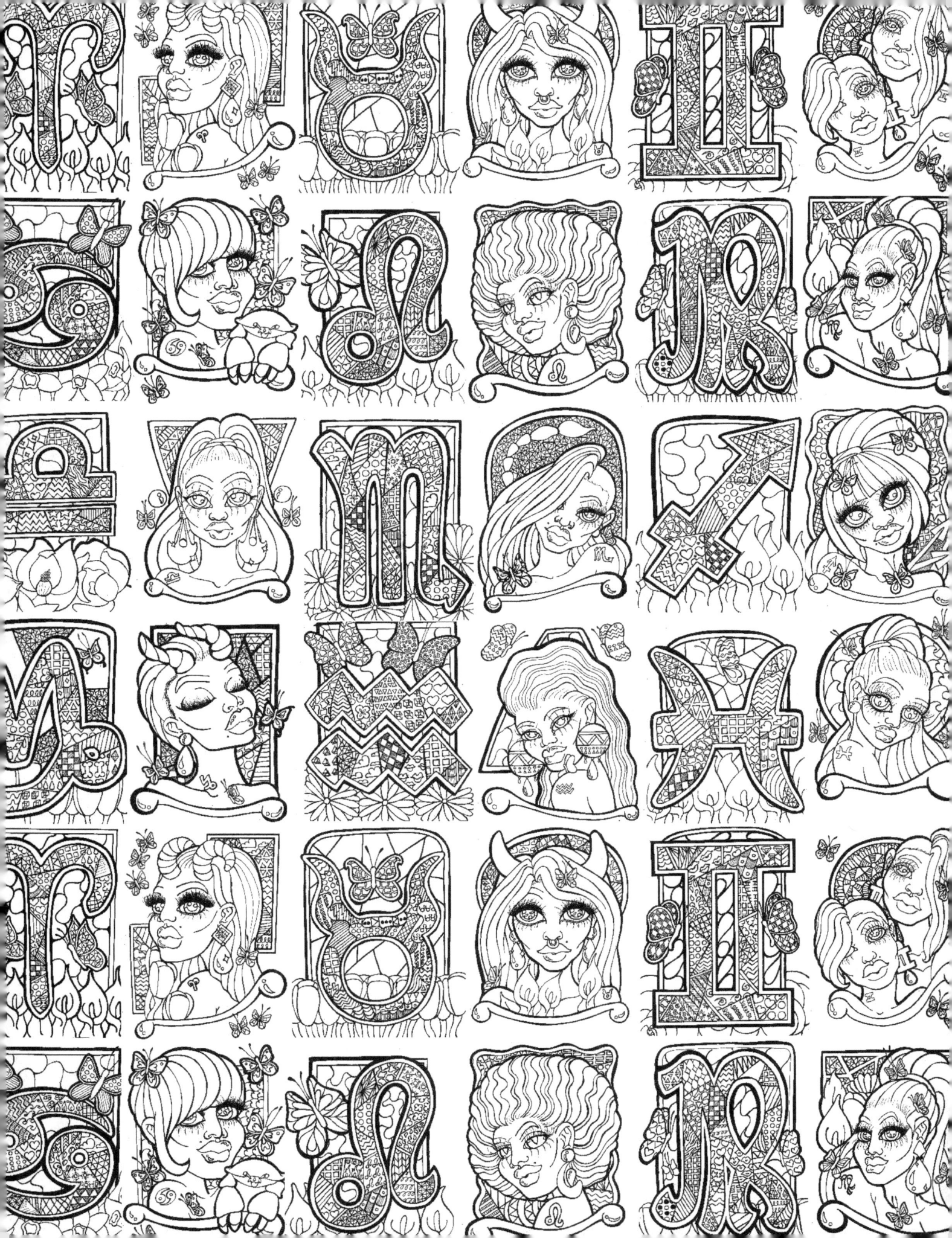

www.ingramcontent.com/pod-product-compliance
Lightning Source LLC
Chambersburg PA
CBHW062158220526
45470CB00009B/2860